PARTNERSHIP MADE

 University
Cheste

D0531343

Russell House Publishing

First published in 2003 by:
Russell House Publishing Ltd.
4 St. George's House
Uplyme Road
Lyme Regis
Dorset DT7 3LS
Tel: 01297-443948
Fax: 01297-442722
e-mail: help@russellhouse.co.uk
www.russellhouse.co.uk

British Library Cataloguing-in-publication Data:

A catalogue record for this book is available from the British Library.

ISBN: 1-898924-88-0

Typeset by TW Typesetting, Plymouth, Devon
Printed and bound in Europe by the Alden Group, Oxford

About Russell House Publishing

RHP is a group of social work, probation, education and youth and community work
practitioners and academics working in collaboration with a professional publishing team.

Our aim is to work closely with the field to produce innovative and valuable materials to help
managers, trainers, practitioners and students.

We are keen to receive feedback on publications and new ideas for future projects.

For details of our other publications please visit our website or ask us for a catalogue. Contact
details are on this page.

Contents

List of Figures

Preamble

Sometimes, being in a partnership can feel like you are in the well-known scenario:

> *Several of you are in a room. It's dark. You take turns to describe what you are holding. You each describe something different. The lights go on. What you each said was something different all turn out to be different parts of a single elephant.*

Others may feel that this reworking of the theme better describes their partnership experience:

> *Several of you are in a room. It's dark. You take turns to describe what you are holding. You each say you are holding an elephant. But when the lights go on it transpires that there are several elephants in the room, and you each have hold of a different one.*

Or this?

> *Several of you are in a room. It's dark. You take turns to describe what you are holding. You each say you are holding an elephant. But when the lights go on, there is no elephant to be found in the room.*

Whatever your particular experience, like the elephant in the final scenario, 'partnership' can certainly be elusive. When, for example, can we say that a partnership has truly come into being? And what exactly do we have to do to make a partnership start?

The difficulty in answering these questions – this elusiveness – is reflected in many people's accounts of what working in partnership is like. Few seem prepared to disagree with the view that working in partnership can be difficult. Many – even those who become successful – find that certain of their partnership experiences can be painful.

This book aims to make you feel as though:

- you are in the same room as your partners
- the lights are on
- the elephants are not white ones
- and none of the elephants – nor your partners – is about to trample on you!

It is principally written to help people and organisations who are working – or thinking about working – inside partnerships.

People whose roles are to impose or encourage partnership working on others – and people whose job it is to manage or evaluate partnerships as a whole, from the outside, as it were – may find things easier after considering what this book sets out to share and explore. But only if they are prepared to learn what it is like to be 'in partnership'.

If you are an experienced partnership worker, you may well have some of the answers to many of the questions raised in this book, and perhaps some of your partners do too. Well done! We hope that you will nevertheless find opportunities when reading this book to reflect on not only what has worked for you, but also how and why. You may also find strength, reassurance and even comfort in learning that others have also stumbled along the way, experienced familiar pitfalls, had feuds, rows and crises that surpass your own – and have gone on to learn from these sometimes painful experiences. We certainly did when asking the many, many questions that made the writing of this book possible.

If you are new to partnership work, or wondering whether to get involved, we hope you will be given the chance to learn from the mistakes that we and others have made in helping along 'the quiet revolution' of joined-up working (Crawford, 1997). What did we do that made partnership go wrong? What did we do that worked? How can we always make sure that everyone involved feels part of the partnership? How do partners celebrate? And so on. If we can spare you some pain, we will have partially succeeded.

But 'surviving' partnership, making it painless, is not enough. Although the demands of partnership working can indeed be of major proportions, the partnership itself is not what concerns our clients or our taskmasters. Partnerships are meaningless unless they improve the services we provide. And partnerships are pointless unless they involve and empower those we are working in partnership to help. A core point of making partnership painless is making these greater goals achievable for more people, more of the time.

A number of case studies appear in the book. Although many are written generically, most are drawn from the experiences of people in youth work, social work, probation, social care, policing, community regeneration and other agencies who work with them in justice, welfare and community settings, particularly health and education. So, the book will be most useful to the people who work in these agencies, whether in government, voluntary or commercial sectors. None the less, these principles of good partnership working can be seen to apply anywhere, regardless of sector or setting.

Just so you know . . .

Case studies in this book draw on the authors' experiences of studying and working in various partnerships. Some resemblance in some of the case studies to individuals or organisations with whom the authors have worked is therefore possible, but the case studies are all fictitious adaptations or extensions of the authors' experiences, and no judgement – or commentary on – their real life partners is implied or intended.

The authors would like to thank all those who have worked in partnership with them for the rich and varied experiences that they have shared. They hope in turn that their partners will find value in the lessons drawn out here from our time spent working together.

Different parts of the book were written by different people, and often in different ways. We invite you to speculate who wrote what, but we may struggle to remember accurately ourselves, such has been the intermingling of our effort and output.

One of our partners on this book had the complex and unenviable task of leading our work in finally drawing together these different parts. Their work has joined them up in a way that has deliberately not ironed out all the differences of opinion and style. Consequently none of the authors would necessarily agree with everything that is written in the book, nor would we each answer in the same way the questions that it raises. But we present it with a shared understanding that partnerships need to make progress, not only in spite of differences, but also in ways that value them.

The Authors

Ros Harrison is a Senior Lecturer in Education at North East Wales Institute of Higher Education (NEWI). She has been a teacher, counsellor and consultant working with public and private sector organisations for over 20 years. Ros worked with the Wales Youth Agency to negotiate a coherent training route for part-time youth workers. This is delivered in partnership between NEWI and twenty-one of the twenty-two Welsh authorities. The purpose of this initiative is to improve the quality of youth service delivery in Wales. As a curriculum framework it also increases access to higher education and has created a career path for participants, enabling them to gain HE credits toward professional qualification.

Geoffrey Mann is Managing Director of Russell House Publishing (RHP) and has been a trustee of the registered charity: Lyme Regis Development Trust. This is his first book. A goal in writing it has been to learn how RHP can maintain and build on its partnerships with authors. In his voluntary work he leads the Trust's work with young people, where his proudest achievement to date has been bringing together, establishing and funding the Lyme Regis Youth Forum. They have been partners with the Trust, the youth service, Connexions, the health service, the drug and alcohol advisory service and other agencies in setting up a youth café in Lyme called InSPARation. In addition he has helped the Trust's work in setting up LymeNET, an IT-based community learning centre, as part of a cross-Dorset SRB-funded multi-agency partnership.

Michael Murphy has been working as a resource co-ordinator for a large childcare partnership (Bolton ACPC) for the last fourteen years. A former member of PIAT (Promotion of Interagency Training) he has published widely in the area of childcare partnership work. Michael has recently moved, as a senior lecturer, to Salford University. As a member of a large family he feels that he does a lot of partnership work at home!

Alan Taylor has been a youth worker, teacher, trainer and a senior manager in a national voluntary organisation. He is currently on secondment to the Prison Service to develop its resettlement strategy. Alan leads on the Service's work with the business and voluntary sectors. Alan has a great deal of experience of developing and evaluating partnerships at national and local level on matters to do with offender resettlement, employment, training and education. He is also the Chair of Russell House Publishing.

Neil Thompson is an independent trainer and consultant with *Avenue Consulting Ltd* (www.avenueconsulting.co.uk). He was formerly Professor of Applied Social Studies at Staffordshire University. He is an experienced author and editor who has written extensively on social work and human relations issues. He now has over 90 publications to his name. Neil is a qualified mediator and has a strong commitment to effective partnership working, conflict management and alternative dispute resolution. He is the editor of the *British Journal of Occupational Learning* (www.traininginstitute.co.uk).

Introduction: Understanding Partnership

Before launching into the main themes and topics of the book, we begin by 'setting the scene' – setting out some of the important issues that have helped to shape the book and our thinking on partnership. Our starting point is the complexity and difficulty of partnership.

Having a bad partnership day?

The first thing to acknowledge is that we have all been there! Things can and will go wrong when we seek to work together in partnership. Indeed, much of the skill involved in partnership work centres on dealing with problems, difficulties, conflicts and tensions. But, an important message of this book is that it is worth persevering with the difficulties – the benefits of partnership can be seen to outweigh the hassles (although it might not always seem like that at the time!).

Given the amount of work that is needed to establish and maintain a healthy partnership it may be useful to outline some of the advantages and disadvantages of working in partnership in order to be clear about what we are dealing with.

The advantages include:

- A focusing of the energies and resources of different agencies on a common problem.
- Enabling a coherent and holistic approach to complex, cross-agency problems.
- Credibility and authority through the involvement of different agencies and the community.
- Access to finance, such as european funding and support from national sources, such as the Single Regeneration Budget (SRB).
- Help in improving the coordination of policy and developing a better understanding of the work of other agencies.
- Help in spreading the responsibilities for taking risks.

And, on the other side of the coin, the disadvantages include:

- A perception of collaboration when the reality can continue to be one of competitiveness and defensiveness.
- Requiring high levels of time, energy and resources to maintain, which small organisations do not possess and which could be used more effectively if directed at the problem itself.
- The promotion of consensus which can lead to the avoidance of difficult decisions.
- The promotion of conflict and the danger that no-one will move beyond this.
- Adopting the culture of the largest agency, or the lead agency, and thereby often not developing cultures that promote the involvement of non-traditional agencies, including agencies operated by minority ethnic groups.
- Too narrow a focus on effectiveness as measured by the achievement of outputs at the expense of a focus on the problem itself.

- The need for people to 'get on' at a personal level – personal relationships are as important as structures.
- The potential for conflicts of interest where some agencies are members of a partnership and also rely on the partnership itself for funding.

Having given a flavour of the pros and cons of partnership work, we now move on to clarify the intended readership.

Who is this book for?

This book is basically geared towards two broad groups of people. First we have those who are thinking about becoming involved in partnership work, whether students in training or existing practitioners who are considering extending their roles and duties into the complex world of partnership. Potentially this is a very broad group but what they would have in common is a need to gain a clear picture of what is involved in working in partnership so that they are better able to equip themselves for the challenges that lie ahead.

The second group comprises the range of people who are already involved in partnership in one way or another. This is also a very broad group, comprising practitioners and managers in statutory, voluntary and private organisations of various shapes and sizes. While people in this second group are likely to be familiar with partnership, there is, of course, still a great deal left to learn for all of us – nobody has all the answers, and we can all benefit by looking closely at the ins and outs of partnership, reflect on the key issues and explore a range of ways of taking things forward. There are many types of partnership, and while they may have much in common, there are also many differences. So, even a person with extensive experience of partnerships is unlikely to have worked across the whole field and will therefore still have uncharted territory to explore and to learn from.

The book may appeal to individuals in either of the two categories described here, but will also be of relevance to organisations across this spectrum, as there is much in the book that could be used to inform organisational policies, strategies and approaches when it comes to partnership.

What is partnership?

Trying to understand how partnerships work can be difficult. It is not helped by the lack of a clear definition of the term, and the enormous variation in the types of association to which the term is applied. On reading the growing amount of literature on the subject, we soon realise that the term seems to be applied to any kind of relationship between different agencies. This book is our attempt to offer to those concerned with forming partnerships (or trying to improve the partnerships in which they are involved) an understanding of what partnership working is about. The content draws from our own collective experiences of working in a range of partnerships relating to employment, youth work, community work, offender rehabilitation, education, social work and social care. We do not, however, focus on any of these specific areas of work. Rather, we concentrate on the common issues that relate to all partnership work.

The current emphasis on partnership can be understood in relation to New Labour attempts to develop a 'third way' – that is, a politics which avoids an over-reliance on both the state (closely associated with Old Labour) and the market (associated with the Conservatives). As Powell et al. (2001) comment:

*Partnership is the **zeitgeist** of the Labour government and one of the essential features of the 'third way' (Hudson, 1999). Documents in a number of fields stress notions of partnership, interagency working, coordination and a seamless service (for example, DoH, 1997, 1998a, 1998b, 1998d, 1999, 2000; DETR, 2000).*

p39.

Sullivan and Skelcher (2002) adopt a similar position in describing partnership as 'the new language of public governance' (p1). They present partnership as the sharing of responsibility with a view to attempting to overcome the inflexibility of boundaries between organisations and across sectors. Partnership, then, has its roots in the developing models of public service provision which have arisen from dissatisfaction with both state-driven and market-led approaches. It is more than just a matter of fashion.

The question of the definition of partnership is a thorny one. Tennyson (1998) defines it as:

. . . a cross-sector alliance in which individuals, groups or organisations agree to: work together to fulfil an obligation or undertake a specific task; share the risks as well as the benefits; and review the relationship regularly, revising their agreement as necessary.

p7.

While this is an impressive attempt to capture the essence of partnership, we have to recognise, of course, that no definition will encompass all that is involved in this very complex type of work. Without doubt, there is a great deal of ambiguity about what is meant by the term partnership. For example, in our conversations when planning this book we realised that some of the authors were using the term 'partnership' to denote just that work done together after the partnership is defined and agreed. But, if this could be called a 'tight' or 'narrow' definition of partnership, others of us were using a 'loose' or 'broad' definition – one that incorporated the work done with partners before

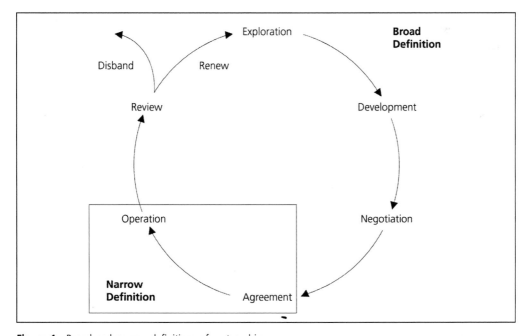

Figure 1 Broad and narrow definitions of partnership.

agreement is reached (exploration, development of relationship, negotiation), while the agreement is in effect, and when it is being wound up.

A review of the literature shows that there is no single, agreed definition and that sometimes the term is used interchangeably with the term collaboration.

Hutchinson and Campbell (1998) point out that partnership and collaboration are terms which are used to describe both the form of organisation and a method of working: 'Having a partnership and working in partnership are very different, but the language can disguise this fact' (p8). At its minimal level partnership can be defined as when two or more agencies come together to achieve more than they can by themselves. However, this definition does not add to our understanding of how partnership differs from other forms of association. The legal definition of a commercial partnership is based on the shared liability of the partners. However, not all partnerships, particularly within social or welfare fields, are legal entities. Sharing liability is however, an important characteristic of many partnerships.

Our aim here, then, is not to attempt to develop a comprehensive definition of the term. Rather, it is to paint a picture of what is involved. It may therefore be more helpful to identify some of the key characteristics that we might expect to see within partnerships generally. In general, successful partnerships:

- Involve more than two agencies or groups, sometimes from more than one sector (private, public, voluntary) and include the key stakeholders – that is, those who are primarily affected by the problem and/or have a responsibility for developing solutions.
- Have common aims, acknowledge the existence of a common problem and have a shared vision of what the outcome should be.
- Have an agreed plan of action or strategy to address the problem concerned.
- Acknowledge and respect the contribution that each of the agencies can bring to the partnership.
- Are flexible in that they seek to accommodate the different values and cultures of participating organisations (see the discussion below of 'valuing diversity').
- Consult with other relevant parties that are not part of the partnership.
- Exchange information and have agreed communication systems.
- Have agreed decision-making structures.
- Share resources and skills.
- Involve the taking of risks.
- Establish agreed roles and responsibilities.
- Establish systems of communication between partners and other relevant agencies.

The existence of these characteristics in a single partnership is, of course, an ideal to aim for, rather than a norm to expect. White and Grove (2000) suggest that four vital elements must exist within a true partnership. These elements are: respect, reciprocity, realism and risk-taking. They argue that, without respect between partners there can be no hope of achieving partnership: 'The essence of *Respect* is the ability to see a person or a party as they really are, not as I or my organisation would like them to be' (pp11–13). *Reciprocity* requires that partners contribute what they can to the partnership: 'If one party has all the power, the finance and the ability to define and label, partnership is absent' (pp11–13). *Realism* 'requires a realistic appraisal of the challenges, tasks and resources' (pp11–13). *Risk-taking* requires that we 'court failure', even though, they argue, this goes against the grain.

These characteristics take time to develop and have to be worked at. They may be more difficult to achieve, at least initially, if the decision to establish the partnership was imposed rather than if it had evolved in response to local needs.

Clearly, then, we have to recognise that we need to work with a fluid definition of partnership. There is no single, agreed definition, although there clearly remains a great deal of overlap in terms of differing perspectives and how the term is used in practice. The potential for ambiguity and misunderstanding is therefore none the less a very real danger to be wary of, and it may often be more helpful to focus on the elements of partnership working, rather than struggle with definitions of 'partnership' as a whole. A suggestion for evaluating the elements of partnership working is offered in Chapter 6.

Teams vs. partnerships

The headline of an article in a March 2000 issue of *Community Care* asked: 'Whatever happened to teamwork?' Yet its author (Greig, 2000; p27) was quite clear in the use of language that at issue were shortcomings in a partnership between two agencies. Though almost self-evidently correct in criticising the poor outcomes of the two agencies' work together – people were clearly suffering as a result – was the author missing the point? Isn't there a difference between teams and partnerships?

To gain a clearer picture of the important differences between the two concepts, we suggest the following distinctions between 'pure' teams and partnerships:

Leadership

Teams have people in charge.

Partnerships have no clear leader, unless they voluntarily elect someone to that position.

Authority

Leaders of teams not only have power over other members of the team, they also have an authority to exercise that power that is independent of the team's members.

No one in a partnership has authority to exercise power over other members, unless members collectively grant that authority.

Exclusion

In a team – to use a sporting analogy – if you play badly, the captain or coach (the leader) can drop you from the next game.

You cannot be excluded from a partnership, no matter how poor your previous performance, unless other members collectively decide to exclude you. Even then, as in a divorce, they may well still have to deal with you.

Purpose

Members of a team have a clear overriding, collective purpose – for example, to win the football game, to save the patient, to boost sales.

Members of a partnership may collectively decide on agreed goals but they do not override their individual goals. So, thinking about the tasks and rituals of partnership has to start from the fact that they bring together individuals and organisations with different goals.

Practice Focus 1

A development trust, which constituted itself as an umbrella for several discrete groups of volunteers, managed a woodland in partnership with a national voluntary agency who wanted to clear out some brambles to encourage the growth of trees and wildflowers. But a trustee who was involved in a community safety partnership lived adjacent to the woodland and reported that their neighbours were given a sense of privacy and security by those very same brambles and were opposed to seeing them cut.

That same trustee was trying to help young people by developing a youth café that gave partnership agencies somewhere to deliver advice, information and counselling. The trustee who was accountable for the woodland advised that they realised that no other suitable building was likely to be found, but that they lived on that street, and were aware of neighbours' already high anxieties about late-night noise from the take-away and Friday night raves and discos.

Striving for a safer community, supporting young people, sustaining the environment – these two trustees and their colleagues had to address conflicting issues not only in the partnerships to which the trust belonged, but also within the partnership of groups that constituted the trust. A lively debate ensued. Was it possible for there to be a successful outcome?

Measures of success

Members of teams will only be deemed successful if they achieve their team goal.

Partners can achieve success as measured against their individual objectives or against their shared objectives.

Let's test the value of these distinctions by looking at a slightly more complicated context. Specifically, are the distinctions offered here between teams and partnerships still valid and useful when a partnership is formed not by different groups acting out of free will, but as a matter of obligation that is imposed by an outside power?

The distinction we are making here is between voluntary and mandatory partnerships. There are many 'mandatory' partnerships. Here are two examples; you may well know of others.

- The Crime and Disorder Act, 1998 requires several independent agencies to form local community safety partnerships, and gives the chief executive of the local authority an executive authority in the partnerships as well. This executive power could be construed as giving them power over the local police, the county council's youth service and other such agencies over which they have no direct management control.

- Other partnerships find themselves bound to act together in certain specific ways as a condition of funding that is supplied to the partnership by large external bodies, such as the National Lottery or the Single Regeneration Budget of the Department of the Environment. In such initiatives, it is often the case that only one agency is accountable to the funding body. In this way, if no other, the accountable agency could be considered to have authority over their partners, while all the agencies, directly accountable or otherwise, have some aspect of their independence compromised by terms and, conditions that are attached to the funding.

Imagine that you are working in such a mandatory partnership:

- Is the obligation that you are under just one of 'being there', or one of 'having to act in a prescribed way'?
- Are you under pressure to show deference to particular partners?
- Which, if any, of the distinctions that we have described between teams and partnerships cease to apply as a result?
- Is there any attempt being made by a large outside body to bring together different agencies into some kind of more formally organised 'corporate' structure, whereby one or more agencies surrender power over aspects of their independence: finances, decision making, policy development, for example?
- Does any such loss of independence affect your entire agency, or just some parts of its operation that relate to the partnership work?

It is worth taking some time to reflect on these matters for yourself – before you read our conclusions.

Conclusions about teams and partnerships

- Although some fairly straightforward distinctions can be offered between teams and partnerships, there are also some more complex, but not unusual, issues that can quite possibly blur the distinctions.
- The questions in the previous section are not always going to be simple for you to answer. Other, similarly complex questions need to be posed when we consider other types of joined-up entities, whether they are teams, partnerships, corporations, mergers or whatever.
- So, true to the spirit of this book, we are not going to answer the questions for you! Rather, we reaffirm our aim of encouraging you to think for yourself in complex situations.
- Our earlier assertion is reinforced: that time spent defining different ways of 'joining together' is of limited value.
- But, looking at the differences between teams and partnerships nevertheless raises important questions with potentially revealing answers that can perhaps inform our 'joined-up working'.

Valuing diversity

'Diversity' is starting to become a new 'buzz-word' – that is, one that is used often, given a great deal of importance, but perhaps not always understood. It refers to the need to recognise that we live and work in a society characterised by an enormous range of differences. The notion of *valuing* (or affirming or even celebrating) diversity relates to the idea that we should appreciate diversity as a positive factor, an asset rather than a problem to be solved (Thompson, 2003a).

The significance of diversity as a factor in relation to equality and social justice has come to be increasingly recognised in recent years. The two major differences between what is now known as 'the diversity approach' and traditional equal opportunities approaches are:

1. The diversity approach focuses on positives rather than negatives. That is, it emphasises the benefits of diversity (cultural enrichment, for example) in the hope that a recognition of such benefits will reduce the amount of unfair discrimination that takes place.

2. Equal opportunities policies have tended to focus narrowly on those forms of discrimination which are illegal. The diversity approach, by contrast, regards any form of unfair discrimination, whether illegal or not, as a barrier to human potential and therefore a problem to be addressed. The diversity approach is therefore much broader than traditional approaches.

Diversity is an important concept in relation to partnership, in so far as partnerships involve people from different backgrounds working together. Valuing differences can be a useful working principle for the diverse interests represented in a partnership situation. Being able to work positively with people whose backgrounds are different from our own is clearly an advantage when it comes to partnership working. It also helps us to keep equality issues to the fore as we go about our business of working together towards shared goals.

Attempts to work in partnership which do not recognise the value of diversity and the need to affirm difference are clearly likely to face far more obstacles than those which are attuned to the dangers of allowing differences to become sources of tension, conflict and communication breakdowns. Approaches to partnership consistent with a philosophy of valuing diversity may well be difficult to implement, such are our strong tendencies to be wary of differences and fearful of the unknown, but they clearly offer far greater potential for success than approaches which ignore the significance of diversity or seek to sweep differences under the carpet.

The importance of partnership

'Why is partnership important?' clearly our answers to this question are major factors in shaping the content and tone of the book. We therefore devote some time here to exploring some of the reasons as to why we need to take partnership work seriously.

The concept of different agencies working together for the common good is not new. What is new, perhaps, is the increased emphasis that recent governments have put on joint working. In the early 1990s the Conservative Government implemented a policy of opening up areas of social and welfare work to market forces and encouraging the involvement of private sector agencies to a greater extent. The Labour Government of 1997 put an even higher priority on partnership working. Its rationale for doing so is based on their view that existing government structures are unable to address effectively many of the current problems faced by society: 'All too often governments in the past have tried to slice problems up into separate packages' (Blair, 1997). The role of the new government is to be one of an 'enabler': 'Whether in education, health, social work, crime prevention or the care of children 'enabling' government strengthens civil society rather than weakening it, and helps families and communities improve their performance . . . New Labour's task is to strengthen the range and quality of such partnerships' (Blair, 1998) This approach was outlined in the government's White Paper, *Modernising Government*, in which it was argued that: 'to improve the way we provide services, we need all parts of government to work together better. We need joined-up government. We need integrated government' (Cabinet Office, 1999). The government's catchphrase was 'joined up problems demand joined up solutions'. See Sullivan and Skelcher (2002) for a detailed discussion of these issues.

Soon after coming to power, the new government established a number of cross-departmental bodies, the most notable being the Social Exclusion Unit (SEU). The purpose of the unit is: 'to help improve government action to reduce social exclusion by producing 'joined up solutions to joined up problems'' (SEU, March, 2000). The importance that the Government accorded the Unit and its work was highlighted by giving it a direct link into the Prime Minister's office.

One of the SEU's early projects was to report on the problems faced by people living in poor neighbourhoods. The Unit set up eighteen Policy Action Teams which included people from a range of government and non-government agencies. Each of these teams was given the responsibility for taking forward a particular part of the work. The report of the team on young people illustrates the Unit's commitment to developing cross-government solutions. It found that existing policy and service delivery on matters relating to young people was fragmented, with at least eight Government departments with an interest in matters relating to young people and several local authority services working directly with young people.

The Policy Action Team considered that many of the problems faced by young people were not being adequately dealt with because of the lack of a co-ordinated response.

> *For decades, no one has had a clear responsibility for making this happen, either in central or local government. This has allowed the increased focus on agencies' individual objectives to lead to less focus on the problems that straddle boundaries. Unless this is addressed, delivery and design of new policies may fall short of what the Government wants to achieve; indeed there is a risk that new initiatives could actually add so much confusion that their underlying goals are seriously jeopardised.*
>
> SEU, 2000; Chapter 5. Section 5.4.

One of the team's recommendations was that there should be a cross-government department approach to youth inclusion and structures to ensure that the government designs and delivers its contribution effectively (SEU, 2000).

Collaboration through partnerships between government and local communities has been promoted as a radical new approach to government. The involvement of communities within these solutions, through consultation and through local representation in partnerships structures, gave solutions a new legitimacy. At the local level new partnership structures were developed to deal with problems concerning youth crime, drugs, unemployment and health. In a relatively short period of time the expansion of partnership working has been so extensive and so rapid that it has been referred to by one commentator as: 'a 'quiet revolution' in the nature and shape of the administrative structures of British Governance' (Crawford, 1997; p55).

The Audit Commission (1999), in a report on economic regeneration, identified the enormous growth in partnership work as a matter of concern. The Commission reported that:

> *In some areas so many of these structures have been set up that the waters are again muddied, and it becomes unclear how overlapping partnerships and strategies actually fit together . . . The*

danger is that the escalating number of partnerships (now supplemented at a regional level) will further confuse regeneration by duplicating each other's functions, and exacerbating 'partnership fatigue' among their members.

Audit Commission, 1999; p57.

The expectation on agencies to attend meetings of an increasing number of partnerships raises issues about the level of resources needed. This is a particular problem for small voluntary organisations, and there is a danger that only the larger organisations will be able to attend the numerous meetings involved. Voluntary organisations should identify the benefits of being involved in a partnership, the resources required and the priority they should give to their involvement. The questions they might ask themselves are:

- Are the aims and objectives of the partnership clear?
- Does the work of the partnership relate to our key aims and objectives?
- What status does the partnership have with other agencies and stakeholders?
- What would be the benefits for our organisation or services users from being involved?
- Are there any disadvantages of being involved?
- How long will it take to realise any benefits?
- What is our current relationship with the other partners or potential partners?
- How might the relationship with other agencies be affected by our involvement in the partnership?
- Will the partnership impact on our existing organisational structures?

There are clearly significant political and organisational issues that have a bearing on partnership, with various forces pushing in the direction of the development of partnership work. However, there are also other sound reasons for taking partnership seriously and giving it the attention it deserves.

For example, it is well recognised that imposed change is the least successful form of change (Kotter and Schlesinger, 1986). Working in partnership is therefore a potentially excellent basis for handling change when it becomes necessary or of promoting change when it is felt to be needed. Indeed, partnerships are often set up specifically to attempt to bring about one or more changes in an organisation, a community or some other network.

If partnership is going to be a sound foundation for effective change, it is important that participants succeed in achieving a sense of ownership. This is needed in order to:

- *Motivate participants.* It is unlikely that participants who have little or no sense of ownership will be strongly driven by a sense of commitment and a determination to succeed. Ownership is clearly an essential basis for motivation.
- *Avoid stress and disillusionment.* Stress and job satisfaction are inversely related (Thompson et al., 1996). That is, the more job satisfaction we get, the less likely we are to experience stress. Partners who do not feel part of the partnership project can easily experience disillusionment, lose job satisfaction and thereby become more prone to stress.
- *Promote joint ownership.* Partnership relies, of course, on joint ownership – a strong sense of shared responsibility for a particular endeavour. Without this, real partnership cannot exist.

Clearly, then, developing a strong sense of ownership is a fundamental part of effective partnership work. How this can be achieved is a major challenge for all involved in setting up and maintaining partnerships, although a lot of partnership working is done when these ingredients are not present.

By using partnership to involve people in change initiatives, both within and across organisations, the process of change can be handled far more effectively and constructively. Bringing people together in partnership can help to identify and consolidate common ground and, it is to be hoped, bring out any underlying tensions or difficulties, so that they can be aired and addressed positively as far as possible. Partnership, then, is very much a vehicle for effective and positive change.

Practice Focus 2

There were strong political and financial imperatives for being in partnership. These sometimes created tensions, given that motivations for being involved varied. The original purpose was therefore sometimes lost, as not all had signed up to the partnership as being a means to the same end – the vision of a better service. Consortia had different levels of commitment to this vision and needed flexibility to enable them to work within flexible parameters. What had not been established was a shared sense of ownership.

Writing the book

The writing partnership

An interesting and significant feature of this book is that it is firmly based on the notion of 'practising what you preach'. That is, the book is in itself the product of a partnership.

It must be unusual, if not unique, to be contacted by the managing director of a publishing company who asks you to join him in writing a book about partnerships in areas relating to social and welfare work. Yet, that is what happened to four of the authors, Neil, Ros, Michael and Alan. Maybe, Russell House Publishing is unusual in that most of its directors have worked in the social or welfare professions. However, Geoffrey, the managing director, has spent most of his career in publishing but, since setting up Russell House Publishing in 1995, he has become an active volunteer and management committee member of several youth and community work projects. It was his involvement in these projects that prompted him to ask some of the directors and authors of Russell House Publishing about their experiences of partnership work. From these discussions he had the idea that Russell House Publishing should publish a book on the issue and invited us to join him as its authors.

Although the five authors have a lot in common in some ways, there is also considerable diversity represented in terms of personal and professional backgrounds, experiences and so on. The simple fact that there were five authors – far more than is usually the case in putting a book together – meant that we had to develop a clear way of working together. And it is important to stress that we worked as a team of authors, rather than simply as contributors to an edited collection.

Given that the book represents five different voices, it is perhaps not surprising that there will be slight changes of style, focus and emphasis in different parts of the book. We could have edited the text rigorously to remove any such differences as far as possible, but this would have gone against our spirit of partnership. The differences in writing style here reflect the different voices within the writing partnership – but these are differences within a context of unity, common aims and shared endeavour.

Indeed, this book is very much a collective effort, in the sense that we have supported each other throughout and faced the challenges of partnership in doing so: keeping the channels of communication open; valuing and motivating each other; handling disagreements and differences of perspective constructively; and so on.

But, as the finished product bears testimony, we did it! We managed to produce a work that we all felt happy with, something that we all felt represented our views, values and approaches. So, for the benefit of any cynics who regard true partnership as an unrealistic goal, the book itself is proof that partnership can indeed work. Whether you feel that the effort was worthwhile is, of course, a matter for you to decide!

Partnerships require high levels of commitment and energy from the agencies and people involved. They can be creative forums for the development of new and exciting solutions to problems, but they can also generate conflicts of interest and power and they can prove highly problematic. The tensions inherent in much partnership work are not limited to what goes on within the partnership, but can impact on the wider work of the agencies involved. But, that is all part of the exciting and important challenge of partnership – to wrestle constructively with the conflicts and tensions and build positively on the solidarity, support and effectiveness of successful partnerships. We have tried to express this both in what the book is trying to say and in the way we have tried to say it – as a partnership in our own right.

The structure of the book

We decided to structure the book in such a way as to start with an introductory section, the role of which is to 'set the scene', to outline the key features of the context of partnership work. This is followed by the major substantive portion of the book. It comprises a fairly detailed account and analysis of the various tasks, processes, helps and hindrances that are part and parcel of working in partnership. It represents our attempt to put forward what we see as the major issues relating to partnership, drawing on a range of practice examples.

We have structured this in a way that broadly represents the chronology of partnership, from tentative beginnings through to consolidation and development, and ending with dissolution or transformation into a new form. In order to represent this process (or set of processes), we have chosen to draw upon an extended metaphor. That is, we present each stage of partnership by analogy with the development of a human relationship. So, we begin with 'The first date' and continue the analogy throughout.

It is important to stress that we are using this extended metaphor as a convenient device to represent the complex processes involved in the development of partnerships. It is a 'teaching tool' and nothing more than that. It is not intended as a theory of partnership development, as we are quite clear that the analogy has its uses, but it also has its limitations and is certainly not sophisticated enough to be presented as a theoretical model or in-depth explanatory framework. It is a tool for getting our message across – a very helpful and effective one, but nothing more than that.

One of the benefits of structuring the chapters of the book in this way is that it gives readers two options. It can be read from start to finish in conventional fashion, with each section building on the insights of the previous ones or, if it is preferred, it can be 'dipped into' in relation to a particular stage or section to suit your needs. This flexibility can be useful in allowing readers to tailor what the book offers to their own needs. You are therefore encouraged to use the book as you see fit, to adapt what is on offer to suit your own purposes or emphases at the time. Indeed, you may choose to use it in one way at one time and then use it differently another time. It is meant to be flexible and 'user-friendly'.

In *Partnership Made Painless* we:

- Put forward our understanding of what is meant by partnerships and partnership work.
- Outline some of the theoretical concepts on which partnership work is based.
- Offer models of development based on forming, maintaining and ending partnerships.
- Identify some of the tasks involved in setting up and operating partnerships.
- Suggest strategies and tips for dealing with some of difficult situations and difficult members that you might encounter.

Wherever appropriate we include examples of partnership work to help highlight a particular point or possible way of working. We hope that readers will be able to identify with the situations we describe and that you will be able to use the advice offered to develop your own strategies for dealing with them.

The book perhaps raises more questions than it answers, but this is only to be expected in a short book that tackles such immensely complex subject matter. We do not apologise for raising so many questions, as it is out intention to encourage and facilitate a critically reflective approach, rather than to provide simple answers. We are well aware of the dangers of proposing simple answers to complex problems, and so we certainly do not wish to mislead anyone into thinking that this is a book that provides cookbook-type recipes for tackling partnership problems. Rather, we hope that our experience, study and reflection in these areas of practice will provide a foundation from which you can develop your own approach.

Of course, in choosing the title, *Partnership Made Painless,* we are using no little irony. Partnerships will never be entirely painless, given the conflicting interests involved and the different power bases which operate, but we are sincere in our belief that what we offer here can help to keep such pain to a minimum – and to maximise the benefits, pleasures and achievements to be gained from rising to the challenge of working in partnership. Finally, but not least, we hope that the book is not without a little humour and that people will gain as much enjoyment in reading it as we did in writing it.

Chapter 1

The First Date: Preparation, Purpose and Planning

Introduction

As we noted in the Introduction, there are many similarities between, on the one hand, partnerships involving people on a relationship level and, on the other, those created by or between organisations. Both involve people coming together with something in common. For the majority of people, it is worth the commitment and energy necessary to build a good relationship. For a significant minority, however, it does not go the distance. So how can you improve the chances of creating an effective partnership?

This chapter looks at the initial tasks involved in building an effective partnership, the processes which help us with these tasks. It also offers strategies for dealing with problems on the way. It includes case examples to illustrate some of the issues. We have written it in such a way that it should be helpful for you, not only if you are beginning a partnership, but also if you have already passed through this stage (in so far as it could still give you insights into how your partnership is working or how it could be improved).

Partnership, whether personal or professional is not, of course, an end in itself. Certainly, professional partnerships are meaningless unless they improve the services we provide. Personal partnerships – or relationships – potentially offer those involved the possibility of something more than individuals may experience alone. Similarly, partnerships between organisations may also offer a combining of resources, both human and material, which ultimately offer more than the sum of the parts. Both types of partnership offer scope for negotiation and some degree of choice. As already noted, White and Grove (2000) identify four elements as essential within a professional partnership: respect, reciprocity, realism and risk-taking. We can recognise these as important features within successful personal relationships. They also need to be embedded within the planning, preparation and processes necessary for effective partnerships across the broad spectrum of social intercourse (we shall revisit White and Grove's four elements in Chapter 2).

So, where do you start?

Before establishing a partnership, it is generally a good idea, where possible, to do some preparation, clarify the purpose of the partnership for those involved and make some plans. The first date involves a number of key tasks – quite apart from choosing where to go and what to wear! Some groundwork will pay off. Figure 1.1 below will help you get started in identifying a number of the tasks which you and your partners may find useful to attend to. Some cultures recognise that time invested before the formalities of 'marriage' are well spent!

If you have been denied the chance to undertake such preparation, perhaps because you are joining late or you are being forced into a partnership by a government initiative, it is still worth

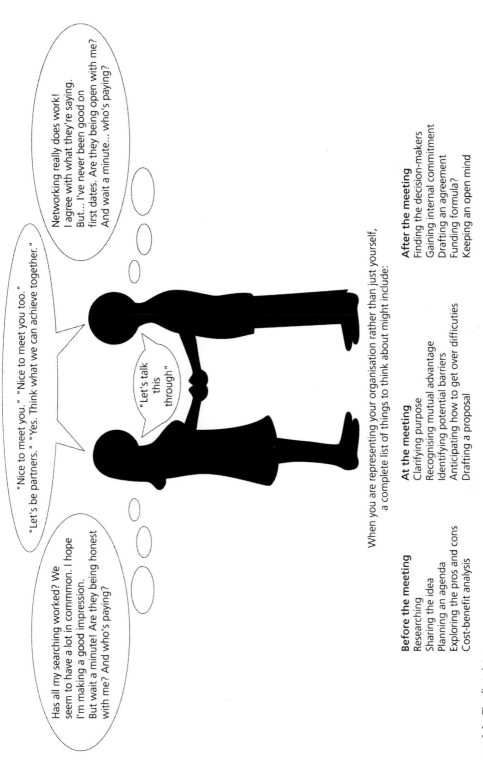

Figure 1.1   The first date

considering the issues raised in this chapter, as it will help you to reflect on what has been missed and how you may be able to compensate.

In clarifying the purpose of the partnership, we are reflecting a time-honoured principle of good practice that applies to so many walks of life – the importance of being clear about what we are doing and why we are doing it. This principle is captured in what Thompson (2002) calls systematic practice. He describes it in terms of three questions:

- What are you trying to achieve?
- How are you going to achieve it?
- How will you know when you have achieved it?

The first question helps us to establish our objectives. The second helps us to be clear about the strategy (or strategies) we are going to use to achieve those objectives. However, perhaps the most important question (but ironically the one that is often neglected) is the third one. This is because it helps us to clarify what success looks like. That is, it helps us to be clear about how we will know whether we have achieved our outcomes. This third question makes sure that we have not been too vague or too general in answering the first two questions. In other words, it helps us to focus.

Thompson's framework of systematic practice can be seen as a useful approach to avoid drift and loss of focus in general, but we would argue that it is particularly relevant to partnership working. This is because the tensions of working within a diverse range of organisations and individuals with perhaps different values, approaches and expectations can easily lead to a situation in which those involved 'lose the plot'. That is, the various tensions can lead partners to lose their focus, and for their efforts and energies to go into taking steps which do not necessarily lead towards achieving the partnership's objectives. In some cases, this 'drift' can be so extreme that, not only are the partners not achieving their objectives, they have completely lost sight of what those objectives are.

There are a number of important processes involved in these tasks. These help us to clarify what we want, why we want it, where and how we may get it and, of course, when.

What we want

It is, of course, really important to clarify the purpose of the proposed partnership. As we have noted, without this initial clarity, it is all too easy to lose focus as the exploration and discussion develop. Each of the partners will have their own expectations and assumptions, based on past experiences (perhaps, initially their own agenda, too). The representatives of the partnership may also, of course, change over time, adding to the complexity of being clear about what we want. So, if the original vision is not clearly articulated, there may be confusion and a loss of commitment. Powell et al. (2001) point out that the government is keen to promote 'SMART' targets. This is a useful mnemonic which we can use to check the aims of the partnership against:

S	specific	Are our objectives clear, specific and not overgeneralised?
M	measurable	Do we have ways of monitoring our progress?
A	achievable	Can we do it?
R	relevant	Do the specific objectives fit with the overall purpose?
T	timed	Are timetables clear, realistic and appropriate?

This also provides a framework for evaluating the potential of a proposed partnership – in other words, do you feel that the first date is worth pursuing?

Practice Focus 1.1

As a college we wanted to establish partnerships between local authorities and ourselves to create a coherent training route towards professional qualification. The vision was a better-qualified workforce capable of improving the quality of the service. The authorities were encouraged to form consortia to maximise their resources. However, the proposals coincided with major local government reorganisation. There was a climate of uncertainty about job security and a lack of clarity about future roles and responsibilities. The vision therefore had to transcend these changes. As the partnerships matured, the processes involved at the beginning sometimes had to be revisited as new players entered the scene. Each new player brought a different history, an alternative script.

Why we want it or 'Your money or your life?'

So often the reasons for creating partnerships tend to be based, at least in part, around potential funding. This is, of course, a strong incentive – maximising your income and moving from a one-bedroomed flat to a three-bedroomed semi! Having someone else to share the everyday ups and downs with. However, there is a real danger in ignoring fundamental differences in values and beliefs which might ultimately threaten the effectiveness – if not the survival-of the partnership. It is useful to explore these early in the relationship. Some ways of doing this are suggested later in this chapter.

When will it come off?

The 'T' in the SMART framework tell us that the aims of the partnership need to be time limited. Individual partners may have different needs in relation to deadlines implicit within the partnership. There may also be different constraints in relation to time available for establishing, sustaining and maintaining the partnership. These need to be shared honestly, so that differences may be acknowledged and agreement reached. It may be that you can only meet for one weekend a month, but you agree to use email and telephone to keep in touch in the meantime.

So, what do you do when things go wrong? The most important strategy is perhaps, the most obvious: keep talking. Communication is, of course, the basis of any good relationship. Language is a wonderful tool, but it can as easily confuse as clarify (Thompson, 2003b). A number of concepts from the literature on interpersonal relationships and organisational transformation may also be useful. Mintzberg (1996), for example, draws attention to the centrality of the communication processes within partnership and warns against viewing partnership as something to be structured and formalised. One implication of this is that, on your 'first date', you should remember to use all your interpersonal skills to the full.

Where do we get it?

An important part of effective partnership is good working relationships between the partners. You are usually off to a good start with people and/or organisations you know. If you are identifying potential partners from existing networks, you have the advantage of being able to base the new on the old. It is to be hoped that you already share at least some values and beliefs, and have a working knowledge of the culture of each other's organisation. All this can be invaluable information at the preparation stage. If you do seek new partners, then you will need to make good use of existing networks. This will minimise the risk of having nothing in common.

Practice Focus 1.2

The strongest partnerships were created on the basis of relationships based on trust and mutual respect. Some were between previously known partners, and some with new partners. A shared understanding of the benefits for clients and staff overcame the inevitable difficulties along the way. The vision of improving the service was shared and sustained. Clear systems and procedures supported good working relationships.

How do we get it?

Figure 1.1 (p15) indicates some of the tasks to be completed during the process of choosing whether to formalise a potential partnership. The financial imperative can, of course, impose unrealistic deadlines. We are then forced to miss out on some of the preparation which will create a good foundation for the future. It should still be possible to take a step back and put the time into this early stage of getting to know each other and agreeing where you want to go and how you are going to get there.

Practice Focus 1.3

Joining the partnership a year after it had been formed meant that there were a lot of assumptions made. We had missed out on the early meetings. Our staff were initially less convinced that it would improve the service in our area. A cross-consortia workshop was arranged to address some of the difficulties that had emerged. It helped clear up a lot of confusion and we came up with some fairly simple solutions to the problems. I think we should have more opportunities like that. It's not the same when you just receive the paperwork in the post.

Searching

Looking around for a potential partner, does, of course, tend to suggest that we know what we're looking for. There are real advantages in going for the boy or girl next door! You have similar backgrounds and you already know a lot about each other. At first sight, you seem to have a lot in common. However, it may be that you have different aspirations. It could be that familiarity blinds you to the need to be aware of what you really require in a partner. Your needs may well have changed, and any potential partnership could be based on mistaken assumptions. Getting together may seem like an easy option, but you know what they say about familiarity!

Researching

It may well be worth the effort of checking out alternatives. Given your ultimate aim of a partner with specific characteristics, why not invest some time thinking through what is important to you first? Attractive as it may seem to choose someone just like you, you may want to look for someone who will complement your strengths, and minimise your weaknesses. Sharing ideas with those you don't know will mean having to be clear. It will also challenge you to explore the pros and cons.

Making calls

Informal networks are a really good way of doing the necessary groundwork. They give us an opportunity of exploring the options. Alternative technologies make this easier than ever and have the advantage of breaking down some of the barriers inherent in more traditional ways of communicating. Within your own 'family' the internal network will be an invaluable sounding board, giving you a chance to get people on your side. Beyond the 'family', you are then able to explore your ideas knowing you have their blessing. You don't need any introductions, and email, for example, tends to lend itself to both openness and immediacy.

Establishing contact

Once you have identified a potential partner, the next step is generally to arrange to meet. There are decisions to make about the venue and the context. Whether the choice is a game of bowls followed by pizza or a hike in the hills with a flask of hot chocolate, the context and time you agree upon will have quite an influence on this first date. You will want to make first impressions count. There may be factors you have not thought of, and so you will need to keep an open mind. However, a potential partner will be impressed that you have clearly thought things through at this stage.

Getting ready

The organisation of this first meeting is all important. Being clear about what exactly you are doing and who is making the necessary arrangements, and being explicit about the purpose of the partnership will provide a forum for all involved to check both different understandings and explore alternatives which might arise from having different agendas. You have an advantage, in that you will tend to have already had time to think through both the possibilities and possible barriers. It will be important to allow potential partners time to do the same. Creating a partnership involves change, and change, though it may have an element of anticipation, is often far from comfortable.

Who's paying?

This can be a bit of a sticking point. So many relationships founder on disagreements about money. Money management can have connotations of power in a relationship. It is a good idea to be up-front about the finances from the beginning. A cost-benefit analysis may not sound very appealing, but it does acknowledge that the realities may be different for each of you. A draft memorandum of agreement will at least create an objective basis for further discussions.

We have looked at some of the tasks around getting together for a first date. Now we turn to some of the processes and strategies which might help us get off to a good start.

Processes

Mintzberg (1996) has suggested that our self-worth is generally based on comparisons with others. When we define ourselves in this way, one danger is that we do so on the basis that we can only succeed if others fail. In other words, if I win, you lose. Or, if you win, I lose. However, for a partnership to be real and not nominal we need to think 'win-win'. That is, we need to find ways forward which allow all parties to benefit, rather than one benefiting at the expense of others.

What we present here is not a comprehensive account of the processes involved in partnership building, as that would be an undertaking of huge proportions. Rather, we settle for the more modest aim of exploring a small number of processes that have a vital role to play in promoting effective collaboration.

Thinking 'win-win'

In any interpersonal encounter there are a number of options open to us. It is important to strive to become more aware of the choices we make and the likely responses we might get, and therefore better able to make alternative choices. If we become aware of the pattern of our communication and the consequences of that pattern, we can choose to change. To understand each other, we need to keep the lines open. Doing that will be dependent upon how we say what we say, and what response we get. What keeps our conversation going, then, will be the response from another person to how we have said what we have just said.

For example, the statement: 'I don't understand how this idea of needing to think 'win-win' will help me' can receive various responses:

> I'll give you some examples.
> Would you like to talk it through now?
> Do you ever try to understand anything I say?
> Why are you always so negative?
> I'm sure you'll get the hang of it, you usually catch on eventually.
> Well that about wraps it up then. Shall we move on?

How would each of these responses leave you feeling? Which of the responses would you have been likely to give?

Thinking about things like this can help increase our awareness of how we communicate, so that we can become better communicators. It also gives us a tool we can use to analyse poor communication. What was said? How was it said? What was intended? When we are talking one-to-one, or when we are in the middle of a meeting, it can be helpful to work out better ways of both understanding each other and of being understood. The way we communicate creates the impression that others have of us. Some talk about this as though they are reading our 'script'.

Organisational scripts

In a similar way, organisations develop a 'script' that has an influence on the feel, or the culture of an organisation. Have you noticed how when you visit an organisation for the first time, your first impressions of the physical environment and the attitudes of those you meet start to tell a story in much the same way as meeting someone new does? This story (or script) is a metaphor for an individual's or organisation's unique history. Its influence is both in the present and in the future. Just as significant events shape us, so they shape an organisation. Going back to our 'first date' analogy, when we go out on this first date, we may take a lot of hidden baggage. This will tend to influence our whole attitude. Are we cautious? Excited? Trusting? If the relationship continues, we may hope that we will gradually unpack some of the baggage, deciding afresh what to keep and what to throw out. We may, for example, have a whole lot of defences in the baggage which have served us well in the past, but are no longer needed. The date might be full of optimism for the future, or there might be an underlying wariness. Both of these feelings could reflect the past rather than the present, yet impact on both the present and the future. Similarly, the beginnings of exploring a work-based partnership will be suffused with aspects of organisational script. If the partnership is created, it too will begin to write its own script. So, where do scripts come from, and how can you ensure that a new partnership has a winning script rather than a losing one?

We have noted that scripts come from the past. How can an organisation, itself merely a group of people with a common purpose, develop a script? In the life of many organisations, there will be influential figures who have established its purpose and core values. These are reflected in the structure and style of the organisation. The organisation itself will also be geographically and culturally situated, and these factors will contribute to its identity and its culture. The name will also be important, just as our individual names, and the reason we were given them, are significant to us. There is generally a story behind them. Finally, beliefs and values, whether religious, educational, professional or philosophical will be an essential part of the organisation's script. But, just as we can change our individual scripts, so can organisations change theirs and the culture of which scripts form an important part. The people who work within an organisation tend to be empowered by becoming aware of the organisation's scripts and their capacity to be part of the ongoing story (see the discussion of the 'organisational operator' in Thompson, 2003a, and/or of 'the reticulist' in Murphy, 1996).

Getting to know you

So, how can you use this idea of script to understand both your own organisation and any possible partner organisation? Each of you will have made some script decisions which seem to make sense of your place in the world. You could try checking these decisions by locating yourselves along the following series of opposites.

My organisation is the kind of place which:

Tends to fail	Is a success
Takes care of people	Shows no concern for people
Is friendly	Is impersonal
Is open	Is secretive
Is serious	Is fun
Welcomes change	Resists change

- Where did these organisational characteristics come from?
- Are these messages any longer useful?
- If you could change the script, what new messages would you want to adopt?
- When are you going to do that?

Once upon a time

The first date is full of possibilities and we have been looking at some ideas which help this stage of a new relationship become a reality. The notion of an organisation having its own history and culture is not difficult to accept when we acknowledge the part our own histories play in one-to-one relationships. If you have found this analogy useful, consider the fairy tale your own organisation represents. Hewson and Turner (1992) offer some examples:

Is it Cinderella, who always gets left to do the drudgery while the others go to the ball? Is it waiting for a fairy godmother to change the situation?

Is it Jack the Giant Killer, full of courage but not very good at planning ahead, and relying on quick wits and fleetness of foot to win over the powerful enemies it encounters?

Is it Sleeping Beauty, waiting for a prince to come and struggle through all the defences to bring everyone back to life with a kiss?

Is it Little Red Riding Hood, wandering through dangerous forests very visibly with her goodies, unable to recognise a wolf when she sees one? Whatever the fairy tale which most closely reflects the organisation we work in and with . . . fairy tales almost always have happy endings.

p100.

If the fairy tale of your partnership is to have a happy ending too, it almost certainly helps then, not only to have a plan and a clear purpose, but also to:

- Prepare for the relationship you want to build with your prospective partner.
- To think about particular relationships, and perhaps most important of all: Who is in charge?

Leadership

It may seem strange for us to be dealing with leadership at the end of a chapter on preparation and planning rather than in a chapter of its own. Leadership is, after all, a widely researched and extensively published topic. Yet here we are giving the subject just a few pages. Why? This is not least because it is indeed a vast topic: leadership in partnerships could certainly merit a book on its own. But, perhaps more importantly, it is because, as Graham (1997) comments: 'Leadership is not a science to be picked up in one book or course, but an art to be learned over time. It's not simply a set of rules to be followed, but an ability to build relationships' (pp11–12, cited in Barnes, 2002; pvii).

We present our ideas on leadership under the heading of preparation and planning, because we feel it is important to have an understanding of leadership (what it is, why it is important, how it works) *before* getting too far into the process of relationship-building (the subject matter of Chapter 2). Clarifying your thoughts about leadership is a good preparation for seeing what part you can play in rising to the challenge of partnership.

Graham's view of leadership as an ability to build relationships is reinforced by the idea, to be presented in Chapter 2, that developing the qualities of partnership within relationships is more likely to be successful if it is done through negotiation, than through a relationship being imposed.

Nevertheless, in many partnerships, a particular agency or person will be given a leadership role from the outset. For example, in an SRB-funded multi-million pound development partnership, a single agency will almost certainly be given the power to draw down funds and the responsibility of pulling all partner agencies together for the purpose of reporting how the funds were spent. In other instances, a particular person's qualification may give them traditional hierarchical leadership. For example, in the Victoria Climbié Inquiry it has come to light that no-one challenged the paediatrician's diagnosis of scabies; because no-one thought it was their place to challenge a doctor's opinion about the health of a child. Laming notes 'a general reluctance . . . to challenge the diagnoses of what they consider to be eminent medical practioners' (Laming, 2003, p321).

Sometimes, such un-negotiated leadership will sit in a partnership alongside negotiated leadership. For example, Burnett and Appleton (2002) have pointed out that 'the Youth Justice Board can *require* that members of a Youth Offending Team attend a training course'. But, they also advise that staff who join such a team without certain specific relevant experience will 'have to *negotiate* in-service training opportunities, such as shadowing experienced members of staff' who thereby take on some aspects of a leadership role, at least for a while.

Leadership as a special relationship

So even when some sort of leadership is present at the outset, leadership in partnerships can be seen as the development of a special sort of relationship. This is true whether you are in a situation where you want to sort out the partnership first and then find a leader or one where you would prefer to sort out the leader first so that they can then sort out the partnership. In view of the fact that partnership necessitates exploration and negotiation to develop appropriate relationships, we wish to make it clear that 'leadership' should not be equated with one particular individual seeking to lay down the law as to how the partnership should proceed. Rather, we see a leader as someone who motivates, or even inspires, others to work towards a shared vision. It is therefore possible to have more than one leader in a partnership – indeed, in some ways, everyone can be a leader.

Leadership in partnership is important, but it is not a substitute for effective partnership relationships. As elsewhere in this book, we want to leave you thinking about leadership in ways that:

- Encourage you to ask questions.
- Chart some of your options.
- Help you think about things that may happen to partnerships once they are under way.
- Question the value of unexamined concepts of leadership in partnership contexts.
- Even ask whether some partnerships actually need 'a leader'.

Since partnership is all about exploring and communicating and negotiating, we are, of course, not going to offer definitive answers. Developing leadership is not a simple matter of following a set of instructions (Gilbert and Thompson, 2002). It is a complex matter that requires us to consider a number of important issues.

Different contexts for leadership

We have already discussed how various types of leadership will be needed in different types of partnership. We used as examples an SRB-funded multi-million pound regeneration programme and a Child Death Enquiry (the Climbié Inquiry). Others might include: an informal partnership of volunteer groups looking after different parts of the local environment; a Youth Offending Team; a Drug Reference Action Group; and so on.

The differences between these partnerships lie not only in their purpose but also in their nature – the set of characteristics that set them apart from other partnerships. As we shall see in Chapter 2, there are various factors that shape a partnership which can usefully be considered in a discussion about the context of leadership.

Different tasks and processes of leadership

It is just as important to identify what tasks and processes we feel need to be 'led' in the sense of someone occupying the 'boss' role. Different solutions can be found, and be dealt with separately, rather than dumping everything in the 'we need someone to take charge' bin:

- *Organisation.* In community partnerships, for example, few people are happy to take responsibility for booking meeting halls, scheduling meetings, posting notices and circulating minutes, but someone has to. Such matters of organisation and administration are important foundations. It is therefore important that proper arrangements are made for administrative assistance to be made available where possible.

- *Diplomacy.* If someone says: 'The meetings are awful. Everyone interrupts each other. We keep going over old ground. We never finish on time', we can reply that a skilled and diplomatic chair can make a real difference without needing to be 'the boss'. After all, the Speaker of the House of Commons is not the Prime Minister, yet both can be seen to be leaders in their own way.

- *Facilitation.* 'Every time it's the same. You think someone is going to do something and then they say they forgot, or didn't realise that was what they were supposed to be doing.' When we hear this, we can remember that clearly designated action points, agreed at the end of a meeting, and recorded in minutes circulated soon afterwards, can be a big help. So can someone going round to lend a hand.

- *Consultation.* There can be concerns that 'we are pushing ahead too far too fast' and that 'we don't know what we are doing.' Some people say that, if you are not sure, you should always ask for advice, perhaps by getting someone to come along and listen, in a meeting of everyone together or talking with you one at a time.

- *Pushing through.* A common thought is: 'Why is it that I can win the debate, but what we agreed is never carried through?' Sometimes we have to take ownership of our own ideas, and either take action on them ourselves, or accept that winning a debate is not the same as forming a team to do what then needs to be done.

- *Pulling together.* Sometimes people lose faith. Perhaps in such situations, we need to ask a partner for help and motivation and, of course, you should be ready to offer help and motivation in return.

There might well be other tasks and processes requiring attention in a partnership. Like these, on examination, we may find that they can be addressed through 'leadership' or through something else.

Different styles of leadership

A review of Barnes (2002) points out that his book 'places heavy emphasis on leading groups in situations outside of the mainstream, where there is no formal position of power' (Gallagher, 2002; pp21–22). So, although it is about leadership in work with young people, it may nevertheless be useful as a concise introduction to theories of leadership in partnership working as well. Barnes (pp10–11) lists the following styles of leadership. We have summarised his descriptions of each of them:

- *Autocratic – tells.* The leader makes all the decisions.
- *Autocratic – sells.* The leader makes all the decisions, but also explains them.
- *Democratic – tests.* The leader makes all the decisions, explains them, and answers questions.
- *Democratic – consults.* The leader presents options and encourages discussion before making a decision.
- *Abdicratic – joins.* The leader presents options and information and then becomes part of the group that makes a decision by consensus.
- *Abdicratic – delegates.* The leader presents information and then lets the group make its own decision, with their help, if requested, and with the understanding that they will get more deeply involved again if something could go badly wrong. As Barnes reminds us: 'Authority can be delegated, but responsibility never can.' (p11)
- *Abdicratic – abandons.* The leader abdicates all authority and all responsibility, either deliberately or though a loss of control. (We have added the word abandons. Barnes did not offer a word here as he advises that abdication is not a choice when leading young people.)

This may seem like an exhaustive list, and perhaps in leadership with young people it is. But we have managed to think of at least two other styles of leadership that can be displayed in partnerships:

- *Leading with no followers.* The leader has top-down imposed authority but lacks the ability to negotiate with the partners whom they are supposed to be leading, yet tells whoever gave them authority that they remain effectively in charge and that everything is just fine!
- *Leading by not volunteering.* The leader achieves their objective by refusing to undertake a task themselves, knowing that someone else will step into the breach. This is a common pitfall for certain people in voluntary groups. It is different from abdicating because the leader remains in the group and gets involved again later, when it is convenient for them.

Perhaps there are other styles too.

Which style suits you? And does it suit each of your partners, your funders and your clients?

Leadership needs

This chapter might have left you with answers to some of or all of these questions. Later chapters will throw up other matters of relevance. But, in our view, partnership is all about thinking, exploring, communicating and negotiating. So, we encourage you to use all of these skills in an assessment of your partnership's leadership needs. This might be to:

- *Identify and locate help.* 'We need to send someone in to drive this partnership forward,' one of my colleagues said about the community-based charity's involvement in the local strategic partnership. 'Can you drive a partnership anywhere?' another colleague countered. After quite a bit of debate, and with a fair bit of calming talk from the voluntary service council officer, we put in the job description: 'Locate an appropriate role for our organisation in the partnership by exploring the development of relationships with each of our partners in ways that are appropriate to our ambitions, our interest in helping others achieve theirs, and an openness to the idea that doing this might develop benefits that none of us can see in advance, all balanced with recognition of our own and our partners' limitations.' We asked the voluntary service council officer if they could help facilitate this, stressing that the charity's trustees were not looking to abrogate their leadership responsibilities by hiring someone to help in this way.

- *Cope with leadership that may seem inappropriate or unhelpful.* The Youth Inclusion Project (YIP) has a project manager, accountable to the voluntary agency running the project, the Youth Offending Team and the Youth Justice Board, and this tends to lead to a lack of clarity about where responsibility actually lies. Although this structure of accountability 'works well at project level . . . it gets messy above this' as a result of the different 'agendas' of the agencies involved and a competition between them to take credit for the YIP's successes. (Pitts, 2002).

- *Work together to address other leadership issues that might arise.* This might include deciding whether you actually want 'a leader', or would prefer to find help in other ways, or just change someone's role. As one experienced partnership worker told us: 'Whatever else the chair needs to do, it is to keep a balance between task and process: too much process, we get happy clappy but no work gets done; too much task, members feel bullied and undervalued.'

All-partner leadership?

But, whatever sort of leadership structures are in place, everyone in a partnership is in some way a leader, representing their agency, its values and clients. So perhaps everyone, when they are developing their relationships in partnerships, needs to think about their own role in these terms:

> It's not merely skills and techniques, but a subjective blend of personality and style. Leadership involves not only the body and mind, but the spirit and character as well: good leaders have the intuition, compassion, common sense and courage it takes to stand and lead.
>
> Graham, 1997; pp11–12.

Graham, as we have advised, is writing about outdoor leadership. Can partnership work be informed by this? Perhaps it can, if we remember that groups on mountains can get lost in clouds, argue amongst themselves about whether to turn back or go on, and then argue some more about which is the right path to follow in the direction that they have chosen. At times like these, someone who leads the group over a cliff, whether by the force of their will or by the exercise of authority vested in them, is of no value at all; whereas people who can help the group assess their options and decide together how they are going to explore them may well give the group a better chance of success.

So, when working in partnership, it is perhaps true to say not only that, to join up our work together effectively, we must strive to understand the nature of our disjointedness, but also that we must strive together to find ways to make progress when the way ahead (or even where we are) is not necessarily clearly understood in the same way by all concerned.

Conclusion

In this chapter we have looked at the tasks and processes involved in taking the first crucial steps towards building effective partnerships and have proposed a number of strategies for dealing with some of the problems that are likely to arise around the time of 'the first date'. We have presented several case examples to illustrate some of the important issues involved. We noted that four elements are essential within a professional partnership, namely: respect, reciprocity, realism and risk-taking.

Partnerships demand time invested in their preparation, the processes involved in setting up and sustaining them and the tasks inherent in their functioning. However, time and energy invested at these early stages should stand us in good stead at later stages in the partnership, as should become apparent in the chapters that follow.

We also commented on the importance of leadership, not in the sense of the leader as a 'boss' who takes charge, but rather as a leader who helps to set a direction and steer the partnership towards it by helping partners to build relationships.

Chapter 2

Developing the Relationship: Communication, Commitment and Consensus

Introduction

Relationships are, of course, at the heart of partnership working. This chapter is concerned with the development of relationships within partnerships. What makes this development so complex and so interesting is that the people involved bring to the relationship not only the perspective of their own organisation, sector or profession, but also their personal perceptions, values and uncertainties. In many cases, those involved are also responsible for ensuring that the interests and concerns of their organisations and professions are taken into account within the operation of a partnership. Trying to balance the interests of the individuals, organisations and professions to achieve the overall aims of a partnership is a delicate management operation.

In this book, we have compared the stages of partnership development with the stages of human relationships leading up to marriage, and possible separation and divorce. The stages which we have identified: The First Date; Developing the Relationship; Tying the Knot; Keeping Going; and Moving On, as in all relationships, do not necessarily follow in a straightforward linear fashion. At any stage in the relationship, crisis and conflict can occur which may bring the relationship to an end or move it backwards or forward to another stage of its development.

In Chapter 1, we looked at planning for partnership; in this chapter we look at developing relationships from the early stages, which are often characterised by uncertainty and apprehension between partners, to the stage when the relationship is established and the partnership is involved in joint working.

The qualities of the relationships we want to develop

The term, 'partnership' suggests a special kind of relationship that is of a different nature and quality from that found in other kinds of organisational arrangements. There are many opinions about what qualities make an effective partnership, but most include trust, respect, honesty, and shared risk-taking. As we noted in Chapter 1, White and Grove (2000) suggest that true partnership will exist only if there is respect, reciprocity, realism and risk-taking, and that respect is the starting point for partnership. We acknowledge that such qualities are usually key features of effective partnership working, but our own experience of working in partnership suggests that they can take time to develop. Unless organisations have already been involved with each other in a positive long-term relationship, the partnership may initially need to establish a basic working relationship from which they can develop the qualities that White and Grove, and others, have identified.

Our own experience suggests that three processes are key to creating the foundation for effective partnerships. These involve organisations in:

- Enabling the people within the partnership to get to know about each other's organisation and to know the people involved both as professionals and as individuals (developing understanding through *communication*).
- Ensuring that all the partners are involved in ways that enable them to make a full and positive contribution to the work of the partnership (promoting engagement and *commitment*).
- Developing a consensual way of working which enables the partnership to develop and implement a joint strategic plan and which will be the basis for dealing with any future opportunities or threats (building *consensus*).

Understanding through communication

Effective partnership working demands knowledge and understanding by the people involved of how their partners work. In the early stages of a relationship between two people, getting to know each other can be a particularly enjoyable aspect of the developing partnership. Similarly, in partnership organisations, colleagues often identify the insights they have gained into the work of other colleagues and professions as something they have particularly valued and enjoyed. In both kinds of relationship an enormous amount of information about each partner is usually communicated in the early stages. Where couples are concerned, this communication is in response to curiosity, interest and a desire to connect with the other's life. The participants are highly motivated to get to know each other well. In organisational relationships, the driving force behind getting to know and understand each other is usually less strong. A more determined and conscious effort is often required. However, the need to get to know each other is no less important. And in both kinds of partnership relationships, an early focus on getting to know each other can prevent unpleasant surprises at later, inopportune times.

Getting to know each other's organisations

It cannot be assumed that, if organisations are already in contact, the people within them have sufficient knowledge or information about each other's work context to develop a relationship. Moore (1992) illustrates this when discussing interdisciplinary relationships in child protection work:

> We . . . take on the values and philosophies of that profession and we take on board the basic concepts and assumptions which form the frame of reference which we use as the set to solve the problems within our own purview. The tools and methods are self-evident to us but not to other disciplines.
>
> p16.

What each member wants from the partnership is one of the most important areas to address when developing knowledge and understanding about member organisations. For example, many organisations, particularly those within the public sector, have to meet some targets or outputs, which can only be achieved with the help of other organisations. These targets can be important drivers for partnership working.

It can be helpful to make reference to targets such as these in the partnership's strategic plan. By doing so, all involved in the partnership are made aware of key drivers. Explicit reference also means that the targets of individual organisations can be taken into account more easily when monitoring the implementation of the plan, and when making any adjustments. This can result in member organisations participating much more confidently, and with greater commitment, in the early stages of the partnership relationship.

Practice Focus 2.1

A senior manager from a health authority at a conference to promote partnership working between the Prison Service and regional health authorities drew attention to the part of the National Health Service Plan that includes targets for the NHS's work with prisoners. He urged those within the Prison Service, in their attempts to develop partnerships with the NHS, to quote the plan back to the NHS, as it is one of the most important drivers of their work with the Prison Service.

It is important for organisations to be aware of those policies of partner organisations that are relevant to the work of the partnership. These can facilitate and shape an organisation's involvement in a partnership. Organisations in the partnership have to be aware of the boundaries of their partners' potential contribution and involvement. Consider at the outset the contribution and the remit of the partner organisations and the extent to which they can meet the needs of the partnership.

Practice Focus 2.2

A partnership was set up between Jobcentre Plus (an amalgamation of the former Employment Service and Benefits Agency) and the Prison Service. The Prison Service had a target for increasing the number of prisoners who obtain employment after release. As a key partner of the Prison Service, Jobcentre Plus had developed a number of initiatives that would enable the Service to achieve its target. However, the remit of Jobcentre Plus allowed it to work only with people who are actively seeking work. This means it could work only with prisoners once they have been released, and not while they were serving their sentence. To many it would have made sense to extend the role of Jobcentre Plus to initiatives with pre-release prisoners, but the boundaries of Jobcentre Plus's remit could not be changed easily. The Prison Service started looking to develop its relationship with other organisations to fill this gap.

Getting to know each other as people

As well as knowing about organisations (what drives them, the targets they aim for, their remit and policies) it is important that the people involved in the partnership get to know each other, both as professionals and as persons. The human component of partnership working is an area that is often given the least attention by managers, or is left to develop itself. There is an assumption that, if the appropriate structures and systems are in place, those involved in the delivery of services will simply get on and work together. In some partnerships, such as those that involve limited interaction between organisations, this assumption may be appropriate. However, in partnerships where there will be a significant level of collaboration between organisations, such as those undertaking joint planning and commissioning, and dealing with the same client groups, there is a need to manage the development of positive relationships between people. The channels of communication need to be established.

People can respond differently to working in partnership; some may be stimulated by the creativity and flexibility that the relationship can offer. Others may find themselves in situations where they struggle due to an absence of teamwork or a clear mandate, and where their professional roles and usual ways of working are questioned. In such circumstances, they can feel threatened or professionally undermined.

Getting to know each other as professionals

Friction between professionals can occur because of a lack of knowledge or understanding of the roles and the different kinds of relationships that different professions have with their clients. A youth worker working in a school illustrates how this can affect a partnership relationship:

> *I've worked in a school for six months now, working with a teacher doing Personal, Social and Health Education (PSHE). It's never really gone well. We agree what we are going to do, and that's fine. It's when she comes to do it the problems start. She is always a teacher. She doesn't form any close relationships with the kids like I do. She is always careful not to reveal anything of herself. I use what happened to me as a way of exploring things quite regularly. I could go on and on, we're just not on the same wavelength.*
>
> Ingram and Harris, 2001; p143.

Youth workers and teachers have different professional relationships with young people and this youth worker has neither acknowledged the differences nor seen the benefits of the two approaches working alongside each other. During the initial stages in the development of a partnership, organisations should seek to identify and explore these differences and identify how they can be exploited for the benefit of service users.

Some professional groups may fear that working in partnership with other professionals could diminish their particular voice or approach. Such feelings may exist particularly amongst staff who are unclear about what it is that their profession brings to a partnership. In these situations work will need to be done by the partnership to confirm the role of the professional group in the partnership and to strengthen the identity and confidence of the professional bodies involved. This is an issue that was highlighted in the report of the Victoria Climbié Inquiry:

> *What has emerged from the Victoria Climbié Inquiry is a story of misunderstandings that led to a failure to protect a vulnerable child. But what has also emerged is the importance of giving due weight to the opinions of all those professionals that come into contact with a child at risk.*
>
> *Everyone in the team needs to have the ability and confidence to question the decisions of others, whoever they are, consultant or nurse, social worker or junior doctor.*
>
> Dobson, 2002; p27.

Every partner is a person

The full range of contributions that individuals can make to partnership development needs to be recognised. People often consider that they will only be valued for the specialist 'expertise' that they bring to a partnership. However, people are more often valued because of the 'people skills' that they demonstrate in their dealings with others and the way in which they help the development of positive relationships. People skills are important in establishing organisational relationships and setting the culture of partnerships (see Thompson, 2002). 'Every partner is a person, not just an organisation' was an observation made at a workshop, organised by the Employment Service, on developing partnerships in the New Deal (Employment Services, 1999).

Relationship building

The individual relationships between the senior managers of partnership organisations can be an important first step in establishing organisational relationships. Their involvement in work on planning the initial stages of a partnership presents them with opportunities for dialogue, and for personal relationships to form, and respect to develop. The personal commitment that senior managers give to a partnership can also be an incentive to the involvement of other staff in their organisations.

However, many other individuals who will be involved in a partnership often do not have the benefit of the early relationship-building that planning the development of partnership brings about for senior managers. Liddle and Bottoms (1994) provide an example of this in their work on crime prevention schemes, which identified different responses to partnership work between different levels of the hierarchy of social workers and the police. 'There were cases where very positive relationships between the police and local authority officers at senior level provide something of a contrast with relations between police constables and social workers "on the ground"' (p53). The provision of relationship-building activities for other workers or volunteers who may not have had much, if any, contact with the other partnership organisations can make a significant difference to the success of a partnership.

A common response to the need to develop effective relationships between people, particularly in multi-professional teams, is to organise staff development activities to enable people from different professions to get to know one another and to improve group dynamics and strengthen team building. While these are traditionally used to develop teams rather than partnerships (see the discussion in the Introduction of the key differences between 'pure' teams and partnerships), we would argue that they can easily be adapted to apply to partnerships. This is because the issues of interpersonal and group dynamics, communication and conflict management are likely to be very significant in both teams and partnerships.

Such activities usually take place away from the participants' place of work, and they focus, for example, on using group dynamic activities to improve communication and decision-making skills; building trust amongst members; and helping them to deal with conflict. Responses to such activities vary; some people value the time spent with other team members, while others may be sceptical about their value and would sooner focus on more practical issues. The reluctance of some team members to participate fully in these programmes can make the activities ineffective. There is also a danger that, in situations where the relationships between members are already poor, the focus on individuals can make matters worse. Those organising such development activities need to bear these considerations in mind and to be cautious about using events such as these as the sole method of developing better working relationships.

Many of these programmes are facilitated by external consultants. Having an outsider facilitate such events can encourage people to open up to someone they do not know and do not have to work with. However, the use of external consultants can be a disadvantage in that outsiders may not necessarily get to know about or understand the tensions that may exist between team members.

Decisions about the kinds of activities that will be most appropriate, and whether or not to use an external consultant, need to be informed by a needs analysis that takes account of the full range of participants. This need not be burdensome or bureaucratic. However, a systematic approach to identifying development needs, and to identifying appropriately matched staff development processes, will benefit the partnership. It is rare that 'off the shelf' solutions are the best buys in these cases.

Getting together

Many partnerships do not involve people working in teams or working at the same site. They involve different organisations seeking to coordinate the delivery of services across wide geographical and professional areas. In such contexts, it is just as important that the people within the partnerships have knowledge and understanding of their partner organisations. In the main this is provided through written information, such as policy and other relevant organisational documents. It is often useful if people from the different organisations come together in small groups to produce protocols and joint delivery procedures for working in partnership. Representatives from each of the organisations might also come together to evaluate the effectiveness of the procedures by reviewing how the partner organisations responded to specific incidents. It can also be helpful to involve people from the different partner organisations in each other's training events.

Partnerships can also learn from the experiences of other partnership developments, particularly those doing similar work. Some partnerships concentrate their energies into making the partnership work and ignore relationships with other external organisations and bodies. However, it is almost always beneficial to avoid operating in isolation. Networks between partnerships and between professional groups support the dissemination of effective practice, and often provide opportunities for further learning and development. These networks exist, or can be developed, vertically – at national, regional and local level – or horizontally between partnerships across regions or professions. Involvement in these networks can help to identify benchmarks and criteria that will be useful in any evaluation of developing partnership relationships.

Commitment

The extent to which organisations and individuals engage in partnerships, and the quality and nature of their contributions, can vary enormously. Partnership working involves complex negotiation processes. A couple starting out on a new relationship may be able to reach swift and easy agreements about practical arrangements. Other aspects of the relationship (for example, whose influence holds sway when) may need to be negotiated over longer periods of time, and in subtle and indirect ways. However, most couples are keen to accommodate the other's wishes and, in healthy relationships, reach a situation where the needs and contributions of each are treated with equal respect.

Organisations in partnership normally do not have the opportunities that are offered by a couple's closeness and motivation to succeed in the relationship, and to reach such understandings and accommodations swiftly. They usually need to take more transparent and direct steps to ensure that all the member organisations are able to make positive contributions in ways that are relevant to their needs, capability and resources. In addition to paying attention to procedures, they need to look at how the structure and culture of a partnership and the motivation of some individuals can affect the contribution of partner organisations. By creating the conditions in which all partners feel comfortable to negotiate, partnerships will also create conditions for the optimum involvement of member bodies and the effective balancing of needs. In this section we explore some of the issues relating to the different ways in which bodies engage in organisational partnerships and the effect that this can have on the health of the growing relationship.

Context and cultures

We have already mentioned that a wide range of organisational relationships can be called a partnership. At one end of the spectrum are partnerships with loose and informal arrangements involving organisations working together, perhaps only slightly more closely than they would normally do. At the other end of the spectrum are partnerships, usually involving public sector organisations, with distinct and formal arrangements for sharing authority and resources and for communicating between partners. The culture within these more developed and complex partnerships is often similar to that within local and central government. This is not surprising as many of these partnerships are led by government agencies and civil and public servants are responsible for establishing and managing them.

The complex arrangements and the culture within government-led partnerships can be a disincentive to involvement for organisations from other sectors. Some private sector organisations find the amount of bureaucracy that is often a feature of these partnerships time-consuming and a drain on the company's resources. Some partnerships involving private sector organisations, such as private-public partnerships concerned with bidding for, and managing, contracts have addressed these issues by setting up specific partnership groups. These groups are responsible for preparing bids and, if successful, managing the resulting projects. Each of the partner organisations contributes resources to the group, including human resources. What is important in many of these partnerships is that the project group is given a high degree of autonomy for making decisions on behalf of the organisations involved. The group is usually separate from the mainstream activities of its partner organisations and the relationships between the organisations are limited to their involvement in the group.

Some small voluntary sector and community organisations consider that the time, resources and skills needed to participate in these more complex partnerships are too demanding. However, they feel that they are 'forced' into participation by government or their funders. They also fear that, by not participating, they will limit their access to vital information and resources that can affect their future, even their survival.

> Voluntary and community groups who were not part of a larger forum or umbrella group expressed their annoyance at the difficulties they had accessing funds or receiving information in relation to the neighbourhood renewal strategy: 'The only people getting into it are the big organisations who receive a lot of statutory funding. We are getting the crumbs'.
>
> Revans, 2001; p12.

Many small organisations believe that their contribution to these partnerships is not valued as highly as that of the large national voluntary organisations. This is because many of the large voluntary organisations have the necessary resources and skills to participate fully. It is argued that the culture of some of the large national voluntary organisations has more in common with government agencies than with small voluntary organisations. Small voluntary sector organisations also find the more informal, less structured and open membership of network arrangements more attractive than complex, formal partnerships. A research project on networks between Area Based Initiatives (ABIs) involved in regeneration found that networking enabled people 'to talk with each other, build trust and do business outside of the formal channels' (Neighbourhood Renewal Unit and Regional Co-ordination Unit, May, 2001, p18). The people involved in ABIs considered less structured networks to be more effective than formal partnerships. Partnerships should ensure that their structures do not exclude organisations that could usefully participate or prevent them from making their full contribution. They need to be flexible in trying to meet the needs of all their partners or potential partners.

Communication needs

Common to the effectiveness of both formal, developed partnerships and less structured networks is the important role of communication. The quality, methods and channels of communication will change in the lifetime of a partnership, and as relationships mature. In the early stages of partnership relationships, assumptions cannot be made about others' information needs, and effective communication, both within and beyond the partnership, is particularly important. Good communication can help to secure greater involvement by making individuals feel included and confident that they are sufficiently well informed to make a useful contribution. It is well worth spending time at an early stage of the partnership project identifying what needs to be communicated, when, to whom and how (minutes, newsletters, meetings and so on). This communication plan in itself also needs to be communicated and monitored, so that the risk of exclusion is minimised, and potential oversights are reduced.

Money can't buy you love

The motivation of organisations and individuals for working in partnership can have a significant impact on the development and quality of relationships. For example, partnerships whose existence is motivated primarily by funding considerations are often considered as being unlikely to develop sustainable relationships. This may not always be the case, but our experience shows that many of the partnerships set up to secure funding, do not continue for very long after the funding comes to an end.

Practice Focus 2.3

There was a lot of communication between the organisations for the three years we had SRB funding. When that came to an end, and the building and the money were placed with one agency for ongoing management, the communication with that agency practically dried up. It's started again now that Connexions money has started to flow, but in ways that reflect the lack of communication in the interim.

When partnerships are focused on securing funding, relationship problems can often arise after the funding has been secured. The management and the administration of funding from sources such as the European Social Fund and the Single Regeneration Budget are complex and demanding; some organisations do not have the expertise or resources to manage this. In many cases, one of the partner organisations, usually the largest, will take on the role of project or finance manager. In these cases there is a danger that the relationship will move from one where the organisations work collaboratively to one which is closer to a contractual relationship, where the funding manager determines the amount of funding that each partner agency will receive.

Just as funding is not usually, in itself, a strong enough motivator to sustain the continuation of a partnership once the funding runs out, partnerships often founder if a funding application is not successful. Funding is, in our experience, one of the most destructive issues that partnerships have to deal with, particularly if the relationships between organisations have not developed. Even where funding is not the main motivating force for a partnership, matters relating to funding need careful management and it is helpful to continually draw attention to other more positive aspects of partnership working. The risks that funding issues can pose for a partnership project need to be carefully analysed by all the key players in the partnership arrangement. This process, together with an assessment of the level of risk and the joint identification of contingencies, can help to minimise the negative impact that funding matters can have, and strengthen a sense of ownership in the project.

Sustaining motivation

In the early stages of a partnership relationship the longer-term involvement of organisations and individuals is secured, and patterns of engagement become established. Given the time and skills demanded for working in partnership, it is often difficult to motivate some organisations and individuals to become involved, or get involved to a level that can sustain a partnership.

The chances of success are usually higher when incentives for involvement in partnership, and the potential benefits for organisations and individuals, are clearly identified prior to establishing the partnership. However, some professionals may be reluctant to get involved in partnership work for personal development reasons. They think that the more generalist skills required by some partnerships will hinder them from developing the more specific skills needed to progress in their profession and will not help them to improve their career prospects. Partnership working often requires people to take on new roles and responsibilities that are different from those that they normally have. It is important to give the time and the opportunity to develop such skills, and to acknowledge and accredit them when they have been gained.

Practice Focus 2.4

We booked the hall, set the agenda so that we would all have time to contribute. Just three out of nine organisations turned up. A fourth came 90 minutes late and we all had to go through everything again. We tried again a month later; two of the four who turned up first came again. The other two didn't. Two new ones came and we repeated what we did at the last meeting. A month later, and it was more of the same. Everyone become disillusioned. We had to work our way through all of that before we could get on with developing what everyone still agreed was a good idea.

Other steps can be taken to make involvement in partnership work more attractive. Staff on secondment with other partner agencies should be given opportunities to maintain contact with the relevant professional bodies to enable them to update their professional knowledge, skills and practice. Their employing organisation should maintain a professional link and continue to include them in staff development programmes. The learning that the person acquires while on secondment should be fed back to their employing organisation. This will help secondees feel that, as a result of their involvement in a partnership, they can make a useful contribution to their employing organisation.

Where organisations and individuals are only able to make a limited contribution, involving them in sub groups or working groups established by the partnership can secure their engagement. Some partnerships establish different opportunities for involving organisations. For example, the structure of the New Deal consists of two tiers: a core group, which is concerned with strategy, and a larger network group concerned with operational matters. The core group usually consists of managers while the network group may be composed mainly of service providers and service users. If this is done, it is important, however, to give those in the operational group the chance to feel that they are contributing to strategy rather than just carrying it out.

Practice Focus 2.5

Paul worked in a small voluntary organisation and was pleased to have been invited to the Drug Action Team conference. When Paul joined one of the workshop groups there was nobody there he knew. No one spoke at first, and so Paul said that he thought the Welsh policy was more clearly thought through and more compassionate than the English one. An argument ensued and the group's feedback to the main conference was thin, to say the least. Paul felt guilty about this until, over lunch, several people told him that they were glad he had challenged policy, as they felt they couldn't out of concern for job security. This made Paul feel better, but it was perhaps significant that he was not invited to the next conference.

Consensus

Partnership requires organisations to work in ways that are different from their usual practice. They have to take account of new needs that are brought to their work by their partners, and to work across organisations for which they have no authority or management responsibility. Partnerships are about establishing agreements with member organisations to work together to achieve agreed aims and objectives. Most partnerships will include organisations and people with very different aims, objectives and needs. In some partnerships, the organisations involved may have a history of joint working and their relationships may be already established. Other organisations may find themselves working together, not through choice, but as a requirement of government policy or their funders. The organisations concerned may view their partners as competitors, competing for limited resources or for the status of being the leading organisation in their field.

Calming nerves

Developing relationships within partnerships is often about the ability to negotiate between the differing needs of organisations. It is usually necessary, during this early stage in the development of the relationship, to calm the nerves and banish the uncertainties that some members might have.

This is a frightening time for staff in local authority social services departments. People who planned a career in local government as social workers or social care mangers are watching the boundaries of their professional environment give way, and their jobs thrown into a multi-agency melting pot, in the hope of alchemising them into the seamless service of everyone's dreams.

Rickford, 2000; p16.

It may also be the case that people working in organisations fear that partnership working could lead to their organisation amalgamating or merging with their partners, possibly resulting in the loss of jobs or even the disappearance of their organisation. Where organisations, or people, feel under threat, they will come to a partnership feeling cautious and will tread tentatively, looking for hidden agendas. They may give their support to the overall principles of partnership, but they will hold back on implementing some of the more contentious issues until they have seen how the relationship develops and what the partnership will mean for their own organisation.

Participation

In part these issues can be addressed by establishing a culture of participation and consensus. This will involve all the partners in:

- Setting the partnership agenda.
- Collecting and giving free access to information, within legal parameters.
- Transparent decision-making process.
- Developing a written strategy which includes clearly identified responsibilities and (as identified in Chapter 1) measurable and attainable, time-related objectives.
- Reviewing the work of the partnership.

To achieve this, the partnership may have to ensure that all organisations are able to participate fully within the partnership. This could mean that the partnership may have to build the capacity of some partner organisations by meeting the expenses of some partners to enable them to attend meetings, sharing the administrative work and developing the skills of the managers in areas such as project and financial management.

During this initial development stage there is a great deal of responsibility on the lead organisation to help develop relationships, but each organisation must also play its part by identifying the risks and opportunities that working in partnership offers. For some – usually large organisations – being involved may mean delegating some of their existing power and authority to the partnership. For others – usually small organisations – being a partner in a major partnership may raise issues relating to their identity as a distinct organisation.

We have already mentioned that negotiation is an important part of partnership working. The manner in which the negotiation is conducted can also help strengthen the relationship within the partnership, in spite of the differences in the needs of organisations. Negotiation is all about taking the 'I' of the individual need and agreeing a 'we' partnership response. Negotiation is also important to the ability to share risk and to collectively agree what type and level of risk-taking behaviour will be sponsored. Where risk taking is collectively seen to be successful this will further encourage closer partnership relationships.

Evaluation

The involvement of all partner organisations in monitoring and evaluating the early implementation of the partnership's planned work can be a very productive way of managing competing interests. It supports the management of relationships and the development of shared ownership of the project. Participation in these processes helps members to keep the wider picture in view and to understand the potential impact of developments on all areas of the partnership. The provision of planned review points can also defuse tensions by giving everyone the confidence that, at regular intervals, there will be an opportunity to stand back from developments and take account of the full range of experience and perspectives in the partnership. It is important, however, that any review is managed sensitively, to avoid professional defensiveness and a culture of blame being allowed to develop. This is explored further in Chapter 6.

Monitoring and evaluation can lead to decision making, and result in new risks and opportunities being identified and modifications made to plans. Without the direct involvement of all member organisations in these processes, there will not be a good understanding of why certain decisions are made. There will be a risk that the perspectives of a few key players will dominate the partnership and will lead it in different directions. The range of expertise and experience that can be drawn on to the benefit of the partnership will be reduced.

Consensus building has the advantage of involving organisations in planning the development of the partnership, participating in the decision-making process and providing the means for resolving conflict through negotiation.

Conclusion

In this chapter we have looked at developing relationships during the early stages of a partnership – from the time when organisations make a commitment to explore seriously ways of working together, to the time when they have experienced time working together, and the relationships between them are beginning to be established. To continue the comparison with human relationships, it is the period of courting and committing to develop the relationship over the longer term. It is also a time when the feelings of some of those involved include uncertainty, apprehension and, occasionally, hostility. But for many, it is also a time of growth and feelings of optimism about the realisation of plans.

It is a stage in the development of a partnership, when organisations, often with different visions, values and traditions, learn to work together and seek to develop a shared identity and common interest. It is one of the most crucial periods in the development of partnerships, because what happens in this period is likely to affect the future effectiveness, and even the survival of the partnership.

We have argued in this chapter that the qualities usually associated with partnership work – respect, trust, honesty and risk taking – take time to develop, and that the stepping stones towards achieving these qualities involve the organisations in getting to know one another, establishing structures which enable each of the partners to make a full contribution to the work of the partnership, and developing a culture based on consensus. It is impossible to state how long this stage of the partnership process might take. We suggest that partnerships that have been established as a result of external pressures rather than as a result of organic growth, will take longer to develop, and will need to pay particular attention to this stage of the relationship.

It is important to recognise that relationships, even during this early development stage, will constantly change as organisations or representatives join or leave, and as the partnership's work changes and develops in different directions. The environment in which a partnership operates will also change and affect the development of that partnership. The relationships that are formed through the partnership may be one the most stable factors in your service:

So amid all the changes, hang onto your existing relationships. If you've got good working relationships, don't let them get away.

McKeown, 2001.

Chapter 3

Tying the Knot: Roles, Responsibilities and Rituals

Introduction

Put together everything we have considered in this book so far, combine it with your own experience, and you will see why partnership often involves being in a state of near constant change, which no single partner can control, and how this can be difficult, frustrating and sometimes painful. So, the desire for one single, managed, comprehensive and lasting change to alter this can be strong.

Couples sometimes reach a point where they either get married or break up. We can identify two such options for major change which have the potential to take a partnership in more-or-less opposite directions. First, there is what we would call the 'tying the knot' option – making the arrangements for your partnership to become more formal and structured. This can apply to such arrangements for an entire partnership or simply parts of a partnership. Second, there is the option of 'moving on' – ending an entire partnership or losing a single partner's role in a partnership that goes on without them. The first option, that of 'tying the knot', forms the subject matter of this chapter, while Chapter 5 focuses on the 'moving on' option. In each circumstance we look at:

- How you can successfully represent your organisation and manage it inside a partnership when it is going through such major change.
- How the stresses and even the pain of achieving major, managed changes can be kept to a minimum while you consider, decide and act on them.

Tying the knot?

In this chapter we explore what is involved in formalising partnership arrangements and, in carefully detailed stages, take you through what is likely to be involved in the tasks and processes of:

- thinking about it
- talking about it
- negotiating it
- acting on it
- celebrating it
- sustaining it
- living with it

Be warned! Some couples find organising a wedding hard work, once the scale of the list of things to do overtakes initial enthusiasm. But for those of you who want to tie an organisational knot – or just assess what's involved – we hope you will find this chapter to be not only a helpful 'wedding checklist', but also a guide to participative reflection on what's involved.

Particular emphasis is given to 'thinking about it', where we provide an analytical framework on which to keep track of your own and your partners' views and ideas at a critical time in your partnership work. It is a core part of our attempt in this chapter to help you by breaking down a large and complex matter into its component parts. In this way, the chapter will enable you not only to work through the process of change, but also to think through whether such a change is likely to be beneficial to you and your partners, in different circumstances and at different times.

Moving on?

This same approach can be used to look at the issues, processes and outcomes involved in changing a partnership by leaving it or disbanding it. But rather than take you through this whole approach once more in detail, Chapter 5 concentrates on just the issues and possible outcomes of pulling down the shutters and walking away.

Read as a whole, Chapters 3 and 5 will help you to make radical change to a partnership, if that is what you want; and evaluate what that is going to be like and whether it may be more of a hindrance than a help. Throughout, we try to strike a balance between, on the one hand, clarifying the issues, tasks and processes of change and, on the other, not making them seem simpler than they really are. Whichever path you choose, Chapter 4 should be helpful, as it explores 'looking after yourself' and your partners.

Making it formal

Inside many partnerships it can be seen that, quite commonly:

- rules are few
- territory is uncharted
- opinions are many
- change is normal

Such, it could be said, is partnership!

We have also seen that, although there are ways to act positively and constructively in such circumstances, many people find this state of affairs confusing and stressful, possibly even painful. This is an example of 'ontological insecurity', the feelings of uneasiness that we can get in situations where we are not sure of what is expected of us or how we fit into the overall scheme of things in a particular set of circumstances (see Thompson, 2000a).

We should not be surprised, therefore, if we hear calls from several sources, including ourselves, for more formalised relationships between partners and a more structured organisation for the partnership as a whole. In this chapter we use the phrase 'tying the knot' to describe the process that such calls initiate. We explore how you and your organisation may choose to act when such calls for knot-tying are made, considered and eventually put into action. We look at:

- *Making a proposal.* We consider the reasons why you or your partners might want to make a proposal for tying the knot in some way.
- *Getting cold feet.* We flag up some of the anxieties that may be aired about possible pitfalls and dangers.
- *Options.* We identify some of the knots that are available.

- *Thinking about it*. We try to help you through the process of deciding whether or not to tie a knot.
- *Tying it*. We explore and map what happens next!

This chapter presents a lengthy discussion and we make no apology for this. These are big issues, the processes are complex, and the outcomes are significant. And, of course, so is looking after yourself at what can be an especially stressful time. In a final section called 'Tying yourself in knots', we also look at some of the potential effects on you as an employee during this stage of partnership work.

Making a proposal

We begin by looking at some of the circumstances in which a request to tie the knot might be made.

In personal relationships the suggestion may be made for several reasons:

- A desire for emotional security.
- A desire for financial security.
- In the hope of resolving uncertainty.
- To gain a greater degree of control.
- To patch up a row.
- To placate parents.
- For the sake of the children.
- In response to legislation that favours marriage over just living together – for example, tax benefits.
- For the public image of one or perhaps both partners.
- Fate: 'since we've been living together for so long, we might as well, I suppose'.

Most of these can be seen to be mirrored in our working partnerships, and they can result in pressure for change that comes from either inside or outside your partnership. Let's consider each of these in turn.

External pressures

Examples of pressure for tying the knot that originate outside your partnership might include:

- *Placating parents*. Criticism can hurt – and goad us into action – whether it comes from people higher up in your parent organisation, but who are not actually involved in your partnership work, or from onlookers who are held to have greater power of thought, such as the Audit Commission or some other evaluator.
- *For the sake of the children*. Whether your partnership's clients are children or some other group, you may be put under pressure to work more closely together for their sake:

    One of the (Children's and Young People's) Unit's main functions is to break down the barriers between Whitehall departments around policies and services for children and young people . . . The government was emphatic from the outset that it wanted the voluntary sector rather than social services or local government to lead on the children's fund.

    Rickford, 2001; p16.

- *Legislation, or the threat of legislation, that favours marriage.* The NHS Plan published at the end of July has promised financial incentives to reward joint working between local authorities and health authorities. (*Professional Social Work*, September 2000; p1).

- *Fate.* Winchester (2000; p8) concluded her assessment of an interview with the chief inspector of the Social Services Inspectorate concerning the impact of government plans for the Health Service: 'The old argument about having lived together for so long that you may as well get married, could well prove irresistible'.

Internal pressures

Examples of pressure for change that originate inside your partnership might include:

- *Financial security.* The small local voluntary agency had managed to open the youth café, but money was going to be a constant headache. The Youth Service were tremendously supportive and a constructive partnership had been built. But the Connexions Service needed a building and they had money.

- *To patch up a row.* That meeting was the last straw. Everything we had worked towards was going to fall apart unless we could agree on how we could avoid such a bitter argument in the future.

- *Resolving uncertainty.* Who was going to take responsibility? How could we be sure that the money would be made available again next year? The negotiations had been nip and tuck over the last few months. Now there was a five year lease to be signed. If one of the agencies was going to take that degree of responsibility, they needed to know where their partners stood.

Getting cold feet

Of course, getting cold feet may not be what happens next. Indeed, since this book is written at a time of considerable uncertainty about how to work effectively in partnership and considerable consequent pain, you and your partners may be strongly tempted to rush to accept a proposal that seems to offer the potential to clarify relationships, end confusion and conflict, and form an ordered state in which progress can be made which improves services for your partnership's clients.

But few of us would say yes to a marriage proposal without thinking through why the proposal was made and what life might be like afterwards. Indeed, if we think of marriages between people, most of us would not have to think long or hard to call to mind some of the consequences of rushing in. It is therefore important that we should consider what might lie behind the reasons for suggesting tying a knot in your partnership, what might need to be done before the knot could actually be tightened, what might go wrong before then and what might go wrong later. With luck this will sharpen our critical thinking, which should be valuable whether we decide to take the plunge and tie the knot, or decide against doing so.

What lies behind the proposal?

Reasons that we have not yet explored for proposing a more formal structure may include:

- *Control.* It has been suggested that local authorities should combine and control Community Safety, Drug Action and Youth Offending partnerships in a single overriding partnership. Does this reflect a sincere belief that the service provision will improve as a result? Or could it be driven by a sense that these partnerships have been taking political control away from local authorities who are therefore trying to reassert their power?

- *Public image.* It has been argued (Pitts, 2000) that the entire new youth justice agenda has been driven by 'electoral anxiety' rather than by clear evidence that it will work in reducing offending, ensuring justice for young people and providing alternative routes out of disadvantage.

It is not our intention to comment on these viewpoints or to fuel the debates of which they are a part. But they do illustrate perhaps that proposals for tying the knot should not immediately be taken at face value or be assumed to be driven by altruism. Other examples can be explored, and contexts can be recognised where proposals are designed not so much to improve a partnership's performance or counter critical evaluations, but to:

- Change the balance of power between central and local government.
- Gain electoral advantage.
- Assert the primacy of one or more agencies within your partnership.
- Give a partnership worker some kind of personal advantage – for example, gain someone kudos with their boss or help someone look good in a job interview.

Practice Focus 3.1

Even though all the partners felt they should take over management of the New Enterprise when the government money ran out, they felt it was just too big a project to cope with. After lengthy discussion and considerable thought about the impact on partners involved in the project, a letter was sent to the partnership co-ordinator. Saying 'no' was not being done lightly, and was being done in plenty of time so that other ways forward could be explored. Yet the letter was not circulated until after the next meeting and, even then, only with a covering minute that seemed to be designed to cast doubt on its sincerity.

Was this an attempt to try to get the partners to think again? Was it just an indicator of heads being buried in the sands of denial? Was it no more than an administrative oversight of a typically overworked and underpaid co-ordinator?

It was not until the next meeting, two months later that it became apparent that the co-ordinator had moved on to a new job at a higher grade. Everyone felt a bit cynical, concluding that he had suppressed the letter to make sure it didn't undermine a claim made in a job interview. But that was what everyone believed to be the case.

Such assessment of partners' (or paymasters') motives may not give you cold feet about tying the knot. It may well, however, give you and your partners cause to think before you act.

Securing commitment, making arrangements

You might also want to give thought to the size of the task in bringing your partners together in a more formal structure, and the workload that might fall on you (or them) as a result. At the very least, we recommend that you:

- Consider the possibility that the process of trying to agree on 'a more perfect union' may mean a period of greater 'politicking' than is happening already in the partnership – at the expense of getting things done.

- Look at this process in some detail by using the 'framework for your thoughts' provided later in this chapter.

Will we get that far?

Given the potential size of the task of formalising your partnership relationship, it is probably wise to assess the chances of reaching the end of the process of tying a knot before you embark on it. It is important to consider:

- Whether you feel capable and committed.
- What kind of support you have from your agency.
- What kind of support you have from your partners.
- Whether you can carry them along if they do equivocate.

What will it be like later?

Finally, in this assessment of some of the consequences of rushing into a more formal marriage with your partners, you might want to ask what your new relationship may be like. Here are some comments that we have heard:

- As in a marriage, the arguments may not end.
- One or more of you may feel submerged in a more rigidly structured partnership.
- Clients may not notice the difference and wonder what the knot-tying fuss is all about.
- With a bigger, possibly stronger partnership established, your critics may have a bigger and easier target to aim at.
- The bigger, more formal structure may be less, rather than more, efficient.
- The bigger, more formal structure may be hard to adapt at a later date, if you do not get it right first time, or when the social or legal circumstances in which you are operating require such change.
- Splitting up with a lover is hard enough; organising a divorce is harder still.
- Tying the knot may actually signal the end of the benefits of partnership rather than the thing that secures them. For example, the opportunity of small organisations to sit at the same table with some of the bigger ones, and to express their views, may be lost – perhaps along with other opportunities and freedoms.

Such visions of your partnership's future after the knot is tied should at least be considered alongside those of 'wedded bliss' or 'a more perfect union' when you evaluate – on your own or with your partners – whether and how you want the knot to be tied.

Options

As a next step in your evaluation of whether to tie the knot, it is probably helpful to consider the range of possible ways in which knots can be tied. In a rough order of increasing control, such knots can be tied between two or more organisations in the following ways:

- Clarification of lines of demarcation.
- Clarification of links and connections.
- Shared decision-making on parts of your combined operations.
- Forming teams of people from different organisations in the partnership to run discrete processes and projects within the partnership.
- Sharing an executive advisory group.
- Sharing an executive.
- A takeover.
- A merger.

No classification system is going to be perfect, and you may well be able to think of other knots in which you have been tied from time to time. But, to help clarify thoughts, let's nevertheless consider in turn each of the options that we have presented:

1. *Clarification of lines of demarcation.* At the most basic level you can agree with your partners that you will 'leave each other alone', perhaps in certain places, perhaps at certain times. For example, as Jacqui Newell, manager of the Pupil Inclusion Unit at the National Children's Bureau comments, in the Connexions service:

   Personal advisers will be dealing with a wide variety of professionals, including teachers, education social workers and parents, and in many cases will have to argue for the young person . . . [But] head teachers will have the final say on whether or not a child is excluded.
   Newell, 2001; p20.

2. *Clarification of links and connections.* In 1998 New Labour published what has become known as 'the compact'. Hunter (2000; p11) reported then Home Secretary, Jack Straw, as saying that this: 'memorandum concerning relations between the government and the voluntary and community sector [would] foster a shared vision of an inclusive, compassionate and active society'. Hunter added that most observers recognised that the true test of the compact would be how it was translated at a local level by individual authorities.

3. *Shared decision-making on parts of your operations.*

   There is no doubt the provision of health and social services to older people currently involves much duplication of effort and unnecessary paperwork. The single assessment process, or SAP as it has become known, is designed to resolve all this.
   Hunter, 2001; p10.

4. **(a)** *Forming teams (perhaps with delegated budgets) to run processes.*

Practice Focus 3.2

The Safer Families Service took staff and resources from the Area Child Protection Committee and the local substance misuse system. The combined operation was to jointly manage and assist those families in which chaotic substance misuse had led to significant concern about the well-being of children. Staff were joined together to assess and work with the families across normal single agency boundaries. The first step was to agree a process by which their previously separate assessments could be run together.

---

4. **(b)** *Forming teams (perhaps with delegated budgets) to run projects.* 'Pathfinder councils are sought to pilot local initiatives to join up services to give pre and early teens and their families real support and help prevent family breakdown' (Email from LGA to its Children Task Group, August 2001).

Practice Focus 3.3

To secure the SRB funding for the community IT-based learning centre, the partners had to form a more coherent group out of the many agencies that had been working towards it as part of a community regeneration partnership. No one was willing to take on a permanent commitment to run the centre at this stage. There was a sense that the community group should do this, and some pressure as well, but there was no time to build a sufficiently committed team of volunteers. So this had to be declined, and a team was formed to run the project instead. The community group retained a strong stake by signing the lease on the District Council-owned premises. This gave them considerable clout, as premises were very hard to find in this town. The Learning and Skills Council were ultimately accountable to the SRB, and so became team leader in many respects, while the county's voluntary service council undertook operational responsibility for the period of the SRB funding. Involvement and input from other agencies – education-business partnership, a local school, careers service, youth service, and so on – were no longer a requirement for the learning centre project to go forward, but they were encouraged to stay in close touch to explore and develop new ways in which we could work together to regenerate the community.

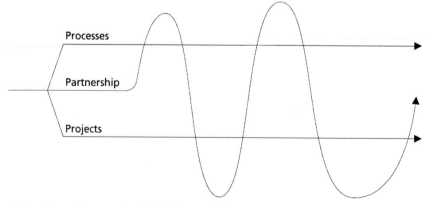

The path of projects and processes should be fairly smooth, if managed properly by a partnership, even if the path of the partnership itself is turbulent. But the interchange and movement of the partnership can suggest checkpoints at which you can evaluate projects and processes, changing their direction if necessary.

Figure 3.1   The paths of projects, processes and partnerships.

5. *Forming a team with specific responsibility for advising the executive bodies of all partners.*

Practice Focus 3.4

The SRB funding covered not only the learning centre in the town but also one at the other end of the county and several other projects as well. There was also a clear hope that all of this would help the partnership work towards other centres and programmes across the county. So, as well as the management team (described above) to run the IT-based learning centre, the local charity became involved in regular meetings to review options for achieving the bigger goal through new initiatives to be developed with all the various agencies involved.

Local strategic partnerships will be between the public, private, voluntary and community sectors and will be responsible for implementing the national strategy action plan at a local level and for contributing to the development and implementation of community strategies. As public services director at the Treasury, Lucy de Groot, said: local strategic partnerships 'would need to have enough punch to ensure that key players were fully engaged in the process'.

Community Care, 15 March 2001; p8.

6. *Sharing an executive (with or without financial control).* This might be either an executive group or a single executive. Wellard (2000; p10) has reported that:

> *. . . commentators have applauded Herefordshire health authority for appointing the director of social services as its new chief executive. Richard Humphries, who holds both posts, is reported to be keen to drop the language of takeover . . . Legally, the health authority and local authority departments must remain separate entities, each with its own accountability arrangements, so a merger cannot go above the level of chief executive or director of services.*

But, as the outgoing chief executive of the local authority explains: 'combining strategic level planning . . . puts us in a better position to deliver on the modernisation agenda.' The journal cites as a specific benefit: 'better mutual understanding and more effective co-operation (on bed-blocking issues). Humphries will be advising both authorities so there won't be the usual mutual recriminations.'

7. *Takeover of management or ownership of an organisation that remains discrete.* Both takeovers and mergers (described below) have clear and significant legal implications. Talk with your legal advisers! In practice, the distinction between a takeover and a merger is not as precise as described here, but it is still useful when we are thinking about our options for developing a partnership. Here is a description of a takeover:

8. *Merger.* This can involve just parts of the organisations involved ' . . . mental health and learning difficulty teams have been integrated and adult team social workers have been relocated to health clinics and GPs' surgeries' (Wellard, 2000; p11). Or it can involve entire organisations: in this, the 'ultimate' in knot-tying, two or more organisations would be merged into a single entity with no obvious recourse for separation. This may involve one organisation merging another into itself and taking complete control. Or it might involve the two organisations combining their assets, liabilities, management structures and accountabilities.

Practice Focus 3.5

To preserve the community theatre, owned and run by the town council, a steering group (answerable to the council) had been set up to explore options for raising funds through a trust, while a council committee continued to have operational control. Following a referendum, the town council pledged to put the theatre into a trust. 'The Theatre Trust Steering Committee was wound up on Tuesday night', the local newspaper reported. 'A new group is now being set up to take the theatre forward to charitable status under the auspices of the Development Trust.' One trustee explained that: this group would take the form of a private company limited by shares. All the shares would be owned by the Development Trust who would therefore have power to appoint and remove directors of the theatre company. But the Trust would be very unlikely to have any other significant role in running the theatre and, theoretically at least, the Trust could sell or gift its ownership of the theatre back to the council or to someone else.

Mergers are not uncommon in endeavours such as publishing (for example, Reed Elsevier, Hodder Headline), media and entertainment (AOL Time Warner) and other areas of business and commerce (Lloyds TSB bank). They are not infrequent in local government (the creation of 'unitary authorities' in England and Wales in the 1990s) or central government (for example, the Department of Transport, the Environment and the Regions). They might prove difficult to achieve in the Third Sector, where the mission of a charitable organisation will quite often be very clearly spelled out, perhaps in its memorandum and articles of association for example, and its trustees may well therefore have clear restrictions on how to dispose of or otherwise reorganise its assets.

Thinking about it

This range of options for structuring your partnership gives quite a lot to think about. Taken together with the number of possible reasons outlined earlier for getting cold feet about such change, it can be seen that thinking about tying the knot will often be complex. And, of course, complex thought can be onerous and possibly painful.

Why think about it? Why not just do it?

One way of avoiding the risk of this particular pain is to duck, not think about it at all, and either 'just go for it' because the need seems so obvious, or because the change to your partnership is being forced upon you. 'Read the plan and just go for it – don't be threatened by it' was the advice from a senior government figure about the NHS Plan that aimed to break down barriers between health and social services, quoted on a front page of *Community Care* (31 August, 2000).

There may be a similar temptation if change is being forced by a coalition of strong partners, or because your organisation is in difficulty. Spending time evaluating the change may seem like a waste of effort. But even if the change is being forced, you will very probably cope with it better if you are able to see clearly what is going on. Perhaps more to the point, the enforced change is unlikely to be so comprehensively planned that every detail of how you and your partners will work together has been sorted out for you.

So, whether you feel that your partnership 'bus' is about to leave with you on it or not, or whether you feel that it is going nowhere unless you drive it, we encourage you to consider the issues raised in the rest of this section.

Why think about it? Why not just focus on your core issues?

A separate option for avoiding the pain is to narrow the field of your thoughts, and stick to a narrow agenda based on self-protection and promotion of your organisation's stated agenda, without regard to wider concerns or the interests of others.

This is not without merit. Letting your thoughts diverge too far can mean a loss of focus, or result in an overambitious agenda that becomes hard to achieve. But looking at the big picture and seeking to understand your partners' agendas can help ensure that you and your organisation have a higher chance of finding support for your agency's goals and of expanding them to the further benefit of your clients. Indeed, it has been argued that, only by having your eyes wide open can you find happiness: 'Knowledge of what is possible is the beginning of happiness', (George Santayana, cited in Chapman, 2000; p20).

Why think about it? Why not trust your emotions?

Issues around tying the knot in partnership work can become as emotional, it sometimes feels, as those that surround marriage. Earlier we looked at the reasons for what can be strong desires to:

- Clarify relationships.
- End confusion and conflict.
- Form an ordered state in which progress can be made.
- Improve services for your partnership's clients.

We have also seen how reasons for not rushing in can be powerful.

Strong emotions are therefore likely to impinge on calm analysis, and they should not be ignored or discounted. They can be powerful signals that we believe what we are saying. They can buy time for us to gather evidence and marshal argument. They can help us to look at things in new ways. But they can also cloud judgement. They can cause those with differing views to 'dig in'. They can prevent us from seeing what we don't want to see.

A framework for your thoughts

So, how can we be clear about our options, plan carefully and channel our emotions and energy into charting the best way ahead? How, at one and the same time, can we keep in mind all these needs? We can:

- Fulfil responsibilities to our:
  - organisations
  - funders
  - co-workers
  - clients
- Endeavour to accommodate the aspirations of partners.

- Be on guard against those of their actions which, although undertaken in good faith, may nevertheless seem to jeopardise our own aims.

No framework for assessment of options in these circumstances is going to work for everyone. What we offer in the rest of this section comes with encouragement not only to use it, but also to assess its value in your particular circumstance first, and then amend it to suit them. With this in mind, we hope this will help you to:

(i) marshal your thoughts before you start negotiations with your partners and

(ii) to keep track of your thoughts once negotiations begin and things start to change.

Remember that it is not intended as a tool for evaluating your partnership as a whole. That is addressed in Chapter 6. Rather, it is offered to help you make the more limited, but none the less crucial assessment of whether or not to make a major and sustained change in your partnership by making it more formal and more structured. It suggests ways to help you consider:

- How things stand for you now.
- Your desire for change.
- Prioritising your needs.
- Your best options for change.
- The change's likely impact on your partners.
- Changes that might work better for them.
- The impact of their preferred changes on you.

The next few pages (Assessments A to G) will probably be hard work. Similarly, organisational change can be hard work. If you wish, feel free to skip over this section and keep reading 'what you can learn from the assessment'.

Assessment A: How do things stand for you now?

Purpose and method

It is difficult to be clear about change, unless you are first clear about what you want to change. One way of doing this is to use SWOT analysis (**S**trengths, **W**eaknesses, **O**pportunities and **T**hreats). Remember that you are assessing not the whole partnership, but how being in that partnership affects your organisation. Here is a quick guide to SWOT analysis, with examples added, to help those of you who may not have used this technique before:

Take a sheet of paper (A4 or flipchart size). Draw a line down the middle and a further line across the centre, so that you have four roughly equal sections. Label the top left-hand box, **S**; the top right-hand box **W**; the bottom left-hand box **O**; and the bottom right-hand box **T**.

Make a record of what, in your current partnership arrangements, are:

S: Current strengths for your organisation

We are a small voluntary organisation. Being in the partnership gives us credibility, especially in funding applications.

W: Current weaknesses for your organisation

We are only a small voluntary organisation. Our partners are big statutory organisations. They have no need to listen to us.

O: Future opportunities for your organisation

There are excellent opportunities to learn from our partners. Even if they only listen to us occasionally, that could make a difference.

T: Future threats to your organisation

We may lose some of our volunteers because having to travel to all the meetings is undermining their commitment and because of the sheer volume of things we are having to respond to.

Doing the assessment

1. Whether you are doing this on your own or with other members of your organisation, start by brainstorming ideas to go into each of the boxes that are provided here. We have given an example in each case.

2. In the first instance write down everything you think of.

3. Then start again with a new set of the four boxes. Copy into them only those ideas that still seem important.

Assessment B: What do you want to change?

Purpose and method

Changing the partnership simply for the sake of changing it is almost certainly not a good reason to make a change – no matter how uncomfortable the partnership politics, no matter how unfathomable it may be to an external evaluator, or how much the elected politicians may want to be seen to be doing something. Ultimately change must be sanctioned by improving services, making them more efficient and more sustainable, and by improving working conditions.

Doing the assessment

1. Record in boxes suggested in Table 3.1 the changes you and colleagues in your organisation would like to make to your partnership.

2. At this point don't worry about whether your partners will agree to these changes.

3. As in the first assessment, start by brainstorming and writing down everything that you and your colleagues think of.

4. Then start again with a new set of the four boxes. Copy into them only those ideas that still seem important. But don't worry if the lists are still long.

5. Try to be as specific as possible. Avoid generalisations such as 'better service' or 'more pay' or 'more money'.

6. Aim to finish up with four lists that represent your 'agenda' before you begin negotiations with your partners about making changes.

It may well help to clarify your thoughts at this stage, if you analyse your desire for change by using a simple table such as this:

Changes I want to make for:	
My clients	
My efficiency	
Sustainability	
My co-workers	

Table 3.1   What do you want to change?

Assessment C: What are your priorities for change?

Purpose and method

Having made the four lists in the previous assessment as the basis of your agenda for negotiation, it is now time to put the contents of each list in priority order, and then to integrate the resulting four sets of priorities. This will almost certainly be a fairly difficult task, as deciding that one thing is 'most important' has the potential to make others seem unimportant. The consequent emotional challenge will be increased when you are doing this exercise in a group with colleagues.

When you subsequently become involved in negotiations with partners, you will almost certainly be challenged, asked to explain why your proposals are important in light of partners' possibly rather different concerns, and expected to show some give and take in the negotiation. So you need to have a point of reference if asked to give up some of your ideas. This is especially true if you are negotiating on behalf of colleagues in your organisation, rather than just yourself, so you know that you are indeed representing all of them, and when it might be important to get back to them before agreeing something with your partners.

This point alone makes it a good idea to keep careful records of this part of your assessment.

You may find it helpful in your own thinking, in discussions with colleagues and then in negotiation with partners if you establish criteria for establishing priorities. For example, you may choose to take into account what seems possible, rather than just what seems to be most needed, or you might want to refer to something like Maslow's hierarchies of need, which many readers of this book may be familiar with (Maslow, 1973).

Doing the assessment

1. Think through whether you have a clear set of criteria on which to base this assessment.
2. If you do, write them down.
3. If you find it difficult to establish criteria, proceed with the assessment anyway, as there will be an opportunity to review criteria later.
4. Look back at the four lists of your agenda for change that you produced at the end of the previous assessment. Write numbers against the contents of each list so as to give them a priority order, with number one as highest priority in each list.
5. Then integrate the four lists into a table such as this. Only one priority should be in each row. Keep going until all priorities from each of your four lists has been included in the table.

6. It is possible that, if your four lists are very long, you will decide during the course of this exercise to focus your attention on a reduced number of priorities. After all, if you have difficulty keeping track of them, your partners will find it even harder; and if they feel that dealing with you is becoming too complicated, they may withdraw rather than engage.

Table 3.2   What are your priorities for change?

Changes I/we want to make . . .	. . . to improve services for clients	. . . to make the provision of services more efficient	. . . to make the provision of services more sustainable	. . . to improve working conditions
Priority 1	All services under one roof			
Priority 2			Clearer responsibilities amongst partners for fundraising	
Priority 3	Services available on more days of the week			
Priority 4				A more open and shared sense of when partners can act in the partnership without reference to the supervisor in their own agency
Priority 5		Less time travelling to meetings		

You may choose to take into account what seems possible, rather than just what seems to be most needed. When you finish it is probably worth revisiting your criteria for making this assessment, whether or not you made these explicit at the start. Reflect on whether your criteria are clear or whether perhaps 'the devil is in the detail'.

Assessment D: What are your best options for making change?

Purpose and method

Having decided on your priorities for change, the next question to be answered must be: How best can we achieve them? Which of the options for tying the knot that we examined earlier in this chapter provide the best chance of delivering the highest number of your prioritised changes?

Our options would include:

- Clarification of lines of demarcation.
- Clarification of links and connections.

- Shared decision-making on parts of your combined operations, granting some kind of restricted authority.
- Forming teams of people from different partnership organisations (with delegated budgets) to run discrete processes/projects within the partnership.
- Forming a team with specific responsibility for advising the executive bodies of all partners.
- Sharing an executive.
- A merger.
- A takeover.

Doing the assessment

1. Start by re-familiarising yourself with these options for structuring partnerships by rereading the earlier section of this chapter in which we examined them. This will be especially important if you are undertaking this assessment in a group.
2. Thinking first of just your overall top priority, write 'yes' or 'no' in each of the boxes of the first column of Table 3.3. For example, is 'clearer demarcation' going to help you achieve your top priority for change: yes or no? What about 'clearer connections': yes or no? And so on down to 'takeover'
3. Then do the same with your second priority in column two.
4. When you have done this for your top five priorities, pause to reflect:

   - Can you already eliminate some of the 'knots' as clearly of no benefit to you?
   - Can you perhaps already see the best way ahead?
   - Whether you think you now have the answer, is it worth continuing this assessment with your next five priorities?
   - Does everyone in your group agree?

5. If there is doubt, we suggest that you keep going with the next five priorities to see if things become clearer.
6. This may seem unhelpful to say now, but you should be alert to the possibility that no clear best option will emerge. If not, it is important that you reflect on this.

   - Are your expectations of what changes might be made unrealistic?
   - Have you got the wrong partners?
   - Do you need to do this exercise on another day, perhaps with other people from your organisation involved?
   - Should you perhaps leave your partnership arrangements as they are?
   - And so on . . .

7. But even though an inconclusive outcome may occur, we encourage you to embark on this exercise in a positive spirit. It might well shed light.

It may help you see a way through what could be a complex analysis to find your preferred way ahead.

Table 3.3 What are your best options for making change?

Is this type of 'knot' likely to achieve:	Priority 1	Priority 2	Priority 3	Priority 4	Priority 5
Clearer demarcation	(Yes/No)				
Clearer connections					
Granting restricted authority					
Process management teams					
Project management teams					
Shared executive advisory					
Shared executive					
Merger					
Takeover					

Assessment E: How will your preferred change impact upon your partners?

Purpose and method

Of course, your preferred way ahead may not be the best option for everyone else.

Arguably it is 'their business' rather than yours to decide what's best for them. Indeed, presuming to know what is best for a partner can be patronising.

However, you will be more likely to achieve your desired outcome if you put some work into persuading your partners, and two key elements of persuasion are being able to show how your suggestions will be of benefit to others, and then overcoming their objections. Thinking this through in advance helps.

Moreover it can be said that successful partners look out for, and try to understand, each other. This assessment could well help in this regard too.

As with our earlier assessments, the goal is to structure and record thoughts, here on how each of your partners might react to your ideas for organisational change, then in Assessment F on what ideas might be in *their* best interests.

Doing the assessment

1. Now that you have decided which particular type of 'knot' would be most helpful to tie with your partners, try completing Table 3.4.
2. Start by writing in the first column how your proposed change will have an impact on you. First do this by referring back to Table 3.2, then add anything else from the lists that you compiled in Table 3.1.

3. Next, write in the box at the top of the next column the name of the partner you think will benefit most from your proposed change, and record 'how' in the rest of the column.

4. Repeat this for the partner who, in your opinion, will next benefit most, and so on until you have completed a column for each of your partners.

As set out here, Table 3.4 assumes you have three partners, A, B and C. If you have more, you will need to add columns.

Table 3.4   How will your preferred change impact upon your partners?

How is this new structure of partnership going to help . . .	My organisation	Partner A	Partner B	Partner C
. . . the clients of:				
. . . the efficiency of:				
. . . the sustainability of:				
. . . the workers of:				

Assessment F: What change might work better for them?

Purpose and method

In the introduction to the previous assessment, we suggested that it can be said that successful partners look out for, and try to understand, each other. There we offered a way to assess how each of your partners might react to your ideas for organisational change.

Now our goal is to structure and record thoughts what ideas might be in *their* best interests.

Doing the assessment

1. Go back to look at how you completed Table 3.4 in Assessment E. The partner whose name you wrote in the last column was the one that you expected to benefit least from your proposed change. Look at what you wrote in the table. Do you still feel that they are the least likely to benefit. If not, who is?

2. Imagine that you are the partner least likely to benefit. Put yourself in their shoes and undertake Assessments A–D for them.

3. If this proves difficult, or if you think that perhaps you are not being objective, try asking an 'independent' person to help you.

4. Repeat this exercise for each of your partners.

Assessment G: How would their preferred change impact on you?

Purpose and method

Once you have completed the probably both difficult and time-consuming Assessment F, you will have developed a sense of which organisational changes to your partnership are likely to be preferred by each of your partners. You probably have a sense of how these changes, which are quite likely to differ from your preferences, will impact upon you. It is important to test this out.

Doing the assessment

1. Which type of organisational change do you think is most likely to be recommended? (Note that this could be because it is the one likely to be preferred by your most powerful partner or the one preferred by most of them.)

2. You can now assess the impact on you of changes that your partners may prefer by using Table 3.4 in Assessment E.

3. First of all do this in a way – or mood – that will develop ammunition for you to obstruct your partners' preferred change.

4. Then, perhaps with the help of an independent adviser, do the exercise again. This time, accept that their proposed change is going to happen. Even if you don't like your partners' ideas, write down how they may nevertheless help.

5. Reflect on which aspects you can accommodate and which cause you and your clients most difficulty.

You can also use this to assess the impact of a change that is being imposed from outside your partnership.

What can you learn from the assessment?

Of course, no system of assessment is likely to give you all the answers, but we would suggest that, in a partnership where you have little if any control over other partners, such an assessment can help you:

- Make decisions about what you most want to achieve in negotiations that lie ahead.
- Achieve the best possible outcome from those negotiations.
- Ensure that you are not left completely out in the cold when other partners are making the knot-tying decisions.

If done with care, and if backed up by a sensible amount of research to help you understand what motivates your partners, the assessment exercises that we have shared with you should help you to identify areas of common interest, grey areas and areas of clear divergence of interest. It is useful to recognise the areas of common interest so that you can identify foundations on which to build.

In almost any kind of work, we all need to spend part of our time in 'comfort zones', where we can get things done in a clear spirit of co-operation. This can recharge our batteries and strengthen positive bonds. But successful partnership workers, like successful explorers, have to venture out into difficult terrain or cross unknown seas. When exploring uncharted territory, you must be ready to try new maps, but also to set them aside and try others when they don't work, perhaps coming back to them if a new piece of knowledge is gained at a later time. In confusing terrain detailed logs work better than memory, which can be fickle at times of stress.

So, although we would not claim that you can rely on thought alone to change your partnership, keeping track of thoughts that have been worked out as clearly as possible is likely to help, as you set out with your partners to navigate the processes of tying the knot.

Tying it

If, after some sort of assessment, you do decide to press ahead with tying a knot with your partners, so that your work together can be allowed to proceed in a more formal and structured context, what happens next? While previous sections of this chapter have looked at options and analyses, this one looks at the processes involved. The stages of a marriage might include:

- thinking about it
- talking about it
- negotiating it
- acting on it
- celebrating it
- sustaining it
- living with it
- getting out of it

In practice, whether in a marriage or a work partnership, some of these things will be going on all the time. Quite often, the sequence may well be different from the 'logical' one presented here. But, even if the process that we have identified is idealised, it nevertheless helps to look at it in these component parts.

Each of these sections could be discussed at much greater length than we have done here. We have deliberately kept them reasonably short so that you can get a feel of the overall process and explore and work out for yourself those issues that may be most relevant to you.

Thinking about it

We have already looked at 'thinking about it' in the previous section. We hope that our efforts were of some help. Only with such clear insight and evaluation is it possible to be an authentic partner when your partnership considers its options for turning proposals for tying the knot into effective action.

But don't stop thinking now! Thought and action, theory and practice cannot easily be separated (Thompson, 2000b). It is important, as you take your organisation through the process of tying the knot that you don't get caught up in a whirlwind, but continue to make time and space for you – and your partners – to think.

Talking about it

Thinking about it is important. But, for a partnership to be successfully structured, unless you are planning a coup, thinking is no substitute for talking. Just as you need to create some thinking space, so too will you be well advised to make room for talk. As we noted in Chapter 2, communication is a central part of relationship building and indeed of partnership more broadly.

How much room? There can be a temptation (perhaps quite legitimately) to make this room big enough for completely free and full discussion. But a recurring theme of this book, in terms of the pains of partnerships, is the demands that they can make on our time.

Also, we have advised that the sections of the 'tying' process don't have clear boundaries, so be careful about taking up too much of your colleagues' time by thinking out loud. Some of that can be useful – for example, by encouraging people to be innovative and creative. But, if it involves too many U-turns, dead ends and incomprehensible flights of fancy, you may alienate people you are trying to draw together. Potentially more damaging would be giving the game away before the negotiation has started.

Here are some *dos* and *dont's* that have been suggested to us for you to think about during the talking time:

Do regard all talking as being, to some extent at least, prelude to negotiation.

Do say that's what you're doing, if you are thinking out loud.

Do set up unthreatening scenarios, if you want to consider some 'what-ifs'.

Do let others have bright ideas, even if you have them first.

Do think about timing: when is a good time to talk? Is now a good time to raise that issue?

Do think about who you want to discuss tying the knot with first.

Do think critically about what others are saying. What might they be holding back? Are they sincere or 'flying kites'? What are they really trying the achieve?

Don't blurt things out without thinking.

Don't claim all the credit.

Don't consume too much of your own or your partners' time.

Don't forget that talking with some partners but not others may make the others worry that you are making alliances at their expense.

Negotiating it

Some of these dos and don'ts could just as easily be written about in this section on negotiation rather than in the preceding one on talking. Indeed, unless you and all your partners are operating under clear shared guidelines, a large element of partnership working at any time involves negotiation:

- How much money can you or your partners put in?
- Who is going to do that task?
- How much time can you spare?
- Whose idea is going to be adopted?

But even if negotiation on such matters never really ceases in your work together, if you are going to take your partnership through the major changes involved in formally tying a knot, there will have to be time and space clearly labelled for negotiating what will be involved.

Improving negotiation skills may be a core training need in a partnership that can be met by either customised or off-the-shelf services. This section can be no substitute for such skills development. Rather it highlights a few points that are special to negotiation in this context:

1. In the two earlier sections of this chapter called 'thinking about it' we have covered one of the absolutely crucial parts of negotiation – thinking about what you want out of the negotiations, and what your partners in the negotiation are likely to want to try to get.

2. When unexpected questions arise, you will also need to be ready to advocate clearly, throughout the process of knot-tying, the values that underpin the service you aim to provide. When that happens, don't be afraid to say: 'I'll need to sleep on it', or that you will have to consult with others in your organisation.

3. But if you do 'withdraw' in that way, take care that you are not raising fears about procrastination: let your partners know what it is that is causing you some doubt, what will be involved in sorting out your thoughts and how long that might take.

4. By the same token, try not to find yourself asking, half an hour after everyone has gone, why a particular individual could not make a commitment on a certain issue. Asking for clarification at the time need not be perceived as threatening by others, nor stressful for yourself.

5. When you do find yourself in agreement on the knot to tie and chart the way ahead, someone must take the time to put an agreement in writing; each of you must share the document with colleagues and advisers.

6. All of you must be ready to come to the next meeting ready to commit, if nothing unforeseen arises and, in this way, show good faith at the point of coming together.

7. But, throughout, 'good faith' must be balanced with 'being on guard', if not for treachery, then at least for oversights.

What should such an agreement say?

It simply is not realistic to expect this book to provide you with some sort of agreement template. You may be able to find a useful model from peers or neighbours who have already attempted something similar to your own particular goals. But you should be ready to learn from their mistakes as well as their successes. More importantly, no matter what the superficial similarities, there will be differences between what you are doing and what others are doing. And, perhaps most importantly of all, cutting short the process of negotiation can all too easily leave things unsaid, apparently shared assumptions untested, and some partners feeling as though they were not consulted. In this last case, they will in all likelihood seek to carry on negotiations after the ink has dried and potentially divert significant time and energy away from getting things done.

But, if we cannot tell you exactly what should be in your partnership agreement, we can still explore the territory with you and, in the next sections, try to chart what you might hope will happen after agreement is reached. In this way, we can describe what might be called 'a basic anatomy' of an agreement, as well as gain insight into how agreements can have a constructive or destructive impact.

Acting on it

Whether the motivation for tying the knot was to build on achievements or to make up for a lack of them to date, after all the effort of setting up a closer and more structured union, it is vital, if credibility is to be maintained, that committed action follows the ending of negotiation.

The first, and arguably most important, action is to ensure that all partners have visibly ratified the agreement and have complete written records of it. If things are then to 'start happening' quickly, the best chances of this will be if several things are defined in the agreement. In this context our 'basic anatomy of agreement' should at the very least cover:

1. *Resources.* Are money, assets (an office, for example) and people's time ready and available? Have the people been properly trained?
2. *Responsibilities.* Do the people know what is expected of them?
3. *Decision-making.* Is it clear not only who will make decisions, but also how issues are to be presented by everyone else?
4. *Timetable.* When does this agreement come into effect? When will it be made public? When will the services that it aims to provide become available?

The sense of urgency can be almost overwhelming, but it may be more important that actions are appropriate, well-presented and sustained, rather than getting off to an early start. Delays can be explained, as long as they are justifiable, and all partners agree on the causes.

If your agreement has been to set up a project of some kind, you may want to refer to a manual on project management or go on a course. Similar guidance can be found on running processes that you might have agreed to adhere to. If it regulates and institutionalises a process for working together in partnership, we would suggest that you keep such advice to hand.

Celebrating it

Let's take a break! Partnership work needn't exclude a bit of fun. More to the point, we have just reached a major, complex and hopefully lasting agreement, and set it in motion. Celebrations of achievements are important, because they:

- Provide a chance to relax a little with the people with whom you have just done all this hard work.
- Signify the change that you hope will now occur in your working relationships with each other.
- Allow you to share the news with others, some of whom may be there to witness your intent to make this change, while others may be invited to hear the good news (your boss, other members of your organisation, politicians, funders, the media – and clients, of course).

But who is paying for the party? This question makes celebration also an early test of how well you can work together. For example:

1. If there has been a 'winner' as a result of the knot being tied, it is an opportunity for them to show their largesse.
2. If there is no clear leader in the newly formalised and structured group, this can get out of hand. As Steven Saylor (1992), creator of Republican Rome's fictional detective, Gordianus the Finder, explained to his adopted son, Meto, in *Catilina's Riddle*:

   In some years rivals are elected, and the stalemate as they try to outdo one another can be spectacular – literally. The year you came to live with me, Crassus and Pompey shared the consulship, and it was one feast after another, festival upon festival . . . the citizens grew fat and saw some fine chariot races.

   p31.

We live in hope!

3. But, if your new arrangements have successfully captured the constructive aspirations of partnership, and you have agreed to a system of shared funding, you should have no trouble sorting out the bills, and no squabbles over who to put on the guest list, and none over who is going to send out the invitations. What does that agreement say?

Have fun!

Sustaining it

With the party over, questions of a similar nature come even more to the fore. However well fed you were at the party, the need for nourishment will not go away. What is in your agreement about providing over time the core elements of sustenance that were seen, in an earlier section of this chapter, to be needed to get started, such as people's time, money and assets?

Of course, times and circumstances change, so the agreement may not be specific on all these matters for an indefinite period – and it will therefore need to be clear about when and how you will review needs, monitor and account for use of resources to date, decide on the amount of these resources to be provided by each partner and who is responsible for seeking further resources from other sources.

Living with it

It may well be that one or more of the partners cannot make clear commitments on sustaining what you have created beyond the current year, let alone indefinitely.

Practice Focus 3.6

No sooner had we set the project up than the Government announced that the lead agency was to be restructured. In retrospect, there was some benefit in thereby being denied some sort of honeymoon, as funding had only been secured for three years. But there would have been some benefit too from a respite from the politics, which now could not happen.

The politics continue. After all this effort to create a more stable environment for working together, it can be exasperating. At such times we can be tempted to turn to some unlikely sources for comfort, or at least advice. Niccolo Macchiavelli wrote in his *Discourses on Livy* (c 1513): 'Those who condemn the quarrels . . . seem to be cavilling at the very things that were the primary cause of Rome's retaining her freedom' (Book 1, Discourse 4) and 'Squabbles . . . should, therefore, be looked upon as an inconvenience which it is necessary to put up with in order to arrive at the greatness of Rome (Book 1, Discourse 6). This, some would say, was the first modern dispassionate political observer trying to make sense of the internecine strife within his beloved Florence and the seemingly interminable wars between the various states of the Italian peninsula: what could be described perhaps as bitter rivalry, spilling over into occasional bloody feuding, that nevertheless produced masterpiece after masterpiece and a search for excellence that produced dynamic change with literary, artistic and scientific monuments that have lasted to this day.

So, maybe it will not be all bad if the politics and partnership wrangling does not go away. What can our agreement say about trying to ensure a healthy face to competition and avoiding the dark sides of consensus that can amount to little more than inertia and fogginess, or even cronyism?

Earlier we looked at the importance of clarity over how decisions would be made and how everyone could present issues. How can you ensure that the decisions will also be transparent, as far as possible at the time they are made, and certainly in retrospect? How can you enshrine the right of all partners for their reasonable requests to be considered? And to whom can they appeal for redress when they feel that a decision was unjust?

Reasonable demands, transparent decisions, redress: are these matters to embed in an agreement? Or are they better left as matters to be sorted out as matters arise in a spirit of partnership that transcends whatever is formalised in an agreement in such a way as to acknowledge competition and value consensus?

Getting out of it

Few of us willingly enter into relationships, with employers, spouses, clubs, magazine publishers, satellite broadcasters (or just about anything else) that we cannot get out of at some point in some way.

As the authors of this book, we entered a contract with the publisher that specified not only what we would strive to achieve together, but also what would happen if one party or other could not do what we had set out to achieve. So, the agreement that ties authors and publisher together in the publishing partnership of which this book is the principal outcome tells us, for example, what could have been done if we had been late in delivering the typescript, what the publisher could have done if they had thought it was a poor typescript, what we could have done if they had accepted it as 'good', but then failed to publish it in a reasonable period of time, what would happen if no-one wants to buy it, what would happen if one of us were to die, or the publisher were bought by another one. This may sound complicated, but it is nothing more than an accumulation of experiences over the years (some good, some bad) resulting in broadly accepted common standards, refined by occasional recourse to legal experts, and shared in a spirit of friendship between peers.

When you look for a template on which to base your partnership agreement, you will do well to look for one that bears such hallmarks, not just with reference to setting up your closer, more structured co-operation, but also reflects how to move on – and out – when the time is right, as needs arise.

There is a lot to think about when considering what many these days call 'exit strategies' – for example, what to do when:

- The money runs out.
- A partnership agency is restructured or closed.
- The timeframe of your agreement has run its course.
- Someone just wants to leave.

In Chapter 5 we look at the issues of 'moving on'. Although written with the principal purpose of letting you consider ending your partnership, you may well find it a helpful way of charting your exits as you put the finishing touches to a closer union.

Towards a conclusion

We have now looked at one way of describing an entire process of tying a knot. What have we learned? Imagine steering your partnership work through the knot-tying process that we have now explored. What is likely to happen along the way? Is it possible to gaze into a crystal ball and reach some sort of conclusion about what it will be like once a knot is tied? Obviously, no-one can ever be sure, and some outcomes will be more likely than others, depending on the circumstances. But, on a few points, we are prepared to stick our necks out and offer the following views . . .

There is a range of reasons for wanting to formalise a partnership. Some of them hold out promise of considerable benefits, but not all proposals to tie the knot should be taken at face value. Certainly all should be thought through carefully – and talked through carefully with your partners. This process of assessment, and then negotiation, can make the problems that you are trying to alleviate worse before they get better – and they may not get better. So, if the impulse to tie the knot is strong, it may well be worth considering a gradual approach. This could involve either tightening the knot gradually (see the Options section earlier in this chapter), or, it could involve tying a knot in just parts of the partnership – perhaps a finite project or process that form a part of the partnership's activities, while leaving partners free to continue to explore other ways of developing their relationship together at the same time.

Certainly, steps towards mergers, whether of whole organisations or just perhaps their executives, should only be attempted with considerable care. Quite apart from issues concerning loss of independence and loss of diversity of voices to speak for different imperatives or needs, the managerial tasks will be complex. At very least, they will almost certainly involve things you won't manage to think of in advance. They may also involve considerable 'personnel problems' including: winning colleagues' support; co-ordinating different terms, conditions and protocols of employment; replacing staff who may be spurred to leave, and other things that you or we may not have thought of. But, if you do decide to tie a knot, however you aim to tie it, and whatever you tie up within it, you should define the knot carefully, in the form of a written agreement, and win all partners' written agreement to it, before you proceed. This will be a lot of work and it may therefore delay achievement of more fundamental objectives.

Throughout the negotiations that preceded formal agreement (and the less formal ones that may well follow it) you will need to strive for a relationship that balances being constantly on your guard and being equally constant in sensitive, constructive partnership behaviours. This is not easy, and so you will need to be able to thrive, or at least cope, at times when things are sometimes far removed from this ideal. This isn't easy either, but these challenges should not necessarily deter partners from considering more formal processes, projects, even organisational structures. For example, not everyone thrives in some of the informal partnership relationships that we have described in this book. More structured working contexts may bring more out of them: a clearly defined role in a clearly defined project run by the less clearly defined partnership, for example. Some projects, such as the acquisition and management of large assets or collective liabilities, may prove impossible for partners whose association is too loose. Whenever one partner's future could be put at risk by another partner's performance or promises, it is usually best to clarify mutual responsibilities in advance.

Given all of this, the personal challenges (and, for some, the pain) can be considerable. These will, in many ways, be no more than variations on the themes explored in the other chapters of this book, but it may nevertheless be worth considering some of these variations, so that you, your colleagues and partners can, if you choose, work to make tying a knot in your partnership as painless as possible.

Tying yourself in knots?

At the end of a chapter that has of necessity been very largely about your organisation and its relationships with its partners, we want to give some time to you. So, in this penultimate section we turn away from work done in partnership on behalf of your employing agency to what this work may be doing to you. Are you thriving in this special and potentially very intense aspect of partnership work? Or are you tying yourself in knots?

Working in partnership can be very rewarding work, but it can also be a significant source of pressure, tension and conflict. It is therefore important that we do not allow these pressures to overspill into stress. There is little point in allowing ourselves to reach the point where stress is preventing us from making a meaningful contribution to the partnership.

While stress is not purely an individual responsibility (there is a significant organisational dimension to stress – see Thompson et al., 1994; 1996), there are things that each of us can do to try to ensure that we do not become overloaded. For example, we can develop a self-care plan in which we try to keep pressures at a manageable level, maximise our coping resources and draw as fully as we can on the support systems available to us (Thompson, 1999). We need to remember that, if we neglect our own needs and thus allow ourselves to become overstretched, then we will be doing our partners no favours – in fact, we could be causing them additional problems.

And finally . . .

As we have seen, the debate about formalising a partnership arrangement is a complex one, as is the challenge of putting such a process into practice. To conclude our discussions of this topic we offer a summary of some key issues by drawing out the parallels between partnerships and personal relationships.

As with relationships, the period leading up to tying the knot can be full of difficulty and anxiety. The crucial thing to remember is that each party to this 'joining' will have a different perspective or view on what is about to happen. These different perspectives can have a profound effect on the final days before the marriage:

- How will you encompass these different views?
- How will you explain your plans to the clients of the partnership?

The arrangements

Because of the differing views on 'tying the knot', making arrangements for the 'joining' can be both practically and diplomatically difficult. Some members of the partnership will want a large ceremony with all the trimmings. Some will want a small registry office with a few witnesses:

- How will you discover what sort of ceremony will best fit your partnership?
- Who do you need to include in working out which arrangements?
- How are you going to keep everyone involved/informed about the arrangements?

Jockeying for position

Before finalising any formal agreement, signatories to that agreement will often engage in jockeying for advantage before the agreement is concluded. Thus, in war, the combatants will often engage in renewed conflict just before a ceasefire, so that the final deal will be advantageous to them. When negotiating the joining contract, partnership members may keep pushing for position right up until the last day.

Stag and hen night

Do not be tempted to arrange final flings before the ceremony. As we shall see in Chapter 4, overindulgences can lead to a crisis or conflict within the partnership.

The perfect day

Remember that the day can never be perfect for everyone. Many participants will have mixed feelings about the marriage. Something in the arrangements always goes wrong. Strive for a 'good enough' day in which a majority of your partnership feel involved.

Happy ever after

This is what happens after the fairy tale wedding. Unfortunately, it is not what happens in 'real life' or in partnerships. In partnership terms we know that tying the knot can lead to a new stage in the partnership, but in this new stage, crisis, conflict and endings are all possible hurdles that the partnership has to contend with. These issues are addressed in Chapters 4 and 5.

Chapter 4

Keeping Going: Care, Crisis and Conflict

Introduction

After couple relationships begin to settle down, there is a lengthy period where the main set of issues is keeping the love alive as the relationship matures. The same can be said of partnerships. This is the stage to where the biggest challenge is to just keeping going or surviving, to see how things go in the coming months. The early struggles to establish viable ways of working together have been successful, but new, critical challenges may now arise.

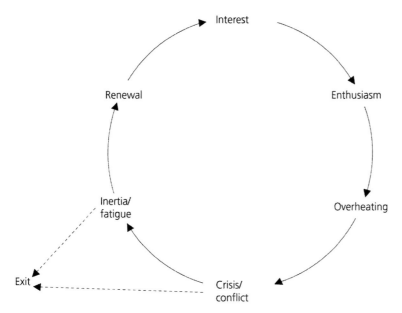

Figure 4.1 The stages of partnership.

In relationship terms, the first phases have been successfully negotiated, but the maturity of the relationship may bring its own problems. In this chapter we outline three crucial issues (care, crisis and conflict) that may arise, and examine the tasks and processes involved in keeping going. We explore which partnership behaviours might help to achieve partnership maturity and which behaviours might exacerbate difficulties at this stage.

The first and most obvious contention is that, within both partnerships and couple relationships, caring, crises and conflicts are a normal part of life (Gordon, 1989). Although crisis and conflict are possible at any time in the life of a partnership, in the early stages partners are usually on their best behaviour and very much 'in love'. In the middle stages, members are enmeshed in the daily drudgery of partnership work, aware of and irritated by, the foibles and weaknesses of their fellow members, and no longer perhaps quite so willing to gloss over difficult issues.

The sign of success is not that the partnership never experiences crises or conflict – no relationship is immune to such things – but, rather, that it has successfully weathered crises and developed ways of dealing with conflict that enable it to carry on operating successfully. If the early stages of partnerships revolve around the formation of psychological and organisational agreements to collaborate, this is the stage where those agreements are revisited to be questioned, shaken and perhaps reformulated. There is a paradox here, in that partnerships are often established to achieve external change in their environment, but frequently find it difficult to achieve internal change in response to things going wrong within the partnership itself.

There are factors in operation within our professional and social environment that are conducive to sustaining partnerships (the most important of which, as we shall see below, is care). These are factors that we can use to promote and enliven our partnership work in the middle stages of its development. However, there are certain other factors (often a mirror image of the first) that act against the successful development of partnerships and will work against the successful continuation of partnership work. These factors may be operating within the partnership or in the external environment but, either way; they have an impact within the partnership.

Care

In partnerships, as in couple relationships, the journey of the participants is often far from smooth. Although we like to imagine that we inhabit a consensual, predictable world, in reality the context in which we live and work is imbued with crises, conflicts and negative occurrences. Were this not the case, the issue of caring could take a back seat in the partnership vehicle. In reality caring needs to ride in the front of the car.

In our current climate the phrase, 'our workforce is our greatest asset' has become something of a cliché, often used just before the announcement of redundancies! But, in partnership terms, the membership and their interactive collaboration *are* the partnership, and this greatest asset needs to be cared for.

Self-care

Partnerships that are undergoing crisis or conflict can often be difficult places to work. It is therefore most important that we begin, before seeking to look after anyone else, to look after ourselves within the partnership (Thompson et al., 1996).

Most partnerships are not set up to achieve personal benefit for their members. The majority are set up in order to achieve some positive outcome for another group of people, another part of the community or the environment. In fact, in many people-care agencies and groups, it is anathema to think of looking after oneself, as this might be seen as being selfish or self-centred. But if we are to make our partnerships work, we must begin by caring for ourselves in order that we can better do our partnership work.

For example, in Practice Focus 4.1 (below), Lisa has reached the stage where she is struggling to be able to resource her partnership commitment. She is doing little to care for herself and as a consequence the whole fabric of the partnership is suffering.

Practice Focus 4.1

Lisa was obviously upset outside the conference room door: 'I can't take it any more, we just keep going round and round in circles'. In the partnership meeting she had just 'lost it' with several other members. She felt completely exhausted. She had been given the role of solution-finder and the reason she had 'lost it' was that, after many weeks of struggling towards a solution of a very complex issue, the group, at the last minute, had come up with a fresh set of problems for her to solve.

Given the importance of self-care, it is essential to consider how you:

- Care for yourself.
- Make sure that you are not over-committed with partnership work.
- Ensure that you are getting something back from the partnership.

Caring for your partners

Good partnerships have a culture of members being able to care for each other. This again is not just because it is 'nice' to be caring, but because a more cohesive, supportive group will be better able to weather crises and conflicts.

Practice Focus 4.2

It had been a difficult meeting for the Phoenix partnership, dominated by organisational conflict. Finbar, recently bereaved, sat quietly on the edge of the meeting. At the end of the acrimonious meeting each partnership member made a point of going up to Finbar, touching him on his arm or shoulder and asking him how he was doing. The group message was clear – no matter how bad the organisational conflict gets, we will still care about each other on a human level.

Care in the partnership context is not about being selfish, being kind to others, or indulging in non-partnership activity. Care is how the group individually and collectively supports partnership work in a human way, as well as in a professional or organisational way.

Crisis

A crisis for the community is not necessarily the same thing as a crisis for the partnership. Indeed some partnerships are set up specifically to deal with community crises and only come into operation in response to those crises (for example, emergency response committees to disasters such as floods, plane crashes and so on). A crisis for a partnership is when an event or imbalance occurs that threatens the future well-being or existence of that partnership. If a partnership has enjoyed relatively uneventful early stages, we may become too confident of our continuing untroubled progress on the partnership journey. At any time, partnerships can be overtaken by unforeseen crises, which we will define as times of intense difficulty or danger, which can threaten the direction or the duration of the partnership.

These crises can have several common causes that we have divided into personal/professional crises and organisational/managerial crises. They can arise from within the partnership or from the external environment. All partnerships (particularly successful ones) are understandably likely to resist change. Of course, what crises always bring in their wake is the fact that change has to be contemplated and negotiated within the partnership.

Personal and professional crises

Partnership fatigue

Partnership work demands patience and energy. As a partnership enters its middle stages, there will be times when, individually and collectively, we suffer from what can be called 'partnership fatigue'. This is the period when we lose sight of the benefits of the partnership and can only see the personal and professional costs to ourselves and our agencies.

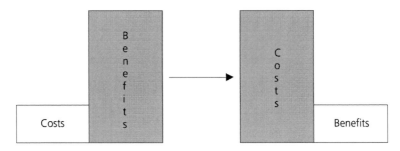

Figure 4.2   Perceived costs and benefits.

At this stage of the partnership we need to ask:

- Why has partnership fatigue set in?
- What can we do to re-energise it – for example, to redistribute the tasks and burdens involved?
- What can we do to care for individual members?

Taken for granted

Within any partnership group, individual members will develop different roles on behalf of the group (leader, solution-finder, problem-spotter, joker and so on). The group will then rely on that member to carry on that role throughout the life of the partnership. Sometimes the group member will feel very burdened by their role and taken for granted by the group.

At this stage we might need to question:

- What roles have we assigned to the different members of the group?
- How might this need to change?
- Who can take on that very difficult role of solution-finder?

Unhelpful roles

Some partnership members may bring 'scripts' (as discussed in Chapter 1) or ways of behaving that the partnership finds difficult to handle, particularly in adversity (we shall discuss this in more detail below). Thus one member may always bring a 'doom is at hand' script that the partnership may find easy (or amusing) to deal with, until something significant does go wrong, when the same script will have a different significance. Another example would be the cynic, the person who has heard it all before and is convinced that nothing is going to work.

Loss and reconstitution

One of the most common forms of crisis at this stage of a partnership is the loss of a member. Members of partnerships frequently form close personal bonds of respect and affection within the group. But these close bonds are often broken by sickness, maternity leave, death or, much more frequently, promotion (positive partnership participants will often be very attractive to other agencies).

Practice Focus 4.3

The New Initiative partnership had been in existence for five years. The community health representative, Lisa, was a very popular, dynamic vice chair. Suddenly Lisa was promoted and had to leave the partnership. Her replacement, Pam, was a very different sort of a person, who was less popular and seemed to give the partnership less priority than Lisa.

Lisa's departure coincided with a major new government initiative. This took the form of increased government demand, immediate deadlines and overcomplex instructions. All of these demands were passed directly on to the partnership. The partnership found it increasingly difficult to keep up with the new demands that were being placed upon it, just at the time when they had lost a key player.

If this is the case, the partnership (often without acknowledging the loss) may go through a period of sadness and mourning, which may be turned into anger against the replacement member. This raises a number of questions:

- How has the loss in our partnership been acknowledged?
- What do we have to change to accommodate that loss?
- Can we let the new member come in and find their own role?

Loss issues are often neglected in organisational life (Moss, 2002), and so it is important to recognise the part that grief reactions can play in partnership working.

Organisational crises

Excessive demand

An organisational crisis of too much demand can occur at any stage of a partnership. However, successful partnerships are often given new tranches of work in their maturity precisely *because* their very success encourages others to insist that they do more (the Early Years development partnerships in the late 1990s are a good example of this). If the partnership is already experiencing crisis or difficulty, it is really important to make sure that this is not compounded with excessive demand (see Practice Focus 4.3 above).

Again a number of questions are raised, such as:

- How can your partnership react to increased demand?

- How can you reinforce your boundaries, reduce expectations or become more realistic in your timescales?

Reduction in resources

This cause of crisis is a mirror image of excessive demand and has the same potential impact on the partnership. Resources alone do not guarantee a partnership's survival or success, but lack of individual or collective resources will always hold a partnership back. In the middle stages of a partnership a sudden reduction in available resources will often cause the crisis (this may coincide with the loss of a member).

Practice Focus 4.4

Pam was the manager who replaced Lisa in the New Initiative partnership, having been asked by her manager to represent their organisation. Unfortunately the meetings of the New Initiative partnership were scheduled for exactly the same time as another partnership where she also represented her agency. She 'managed' by attending one partnership one month (and missing the other) and then attending the other the next month. Both partnerships doubted her commitment and her ability. The New Initiative partnership had been set up with a predominance of representatives from one agency and only one representative (Lisa) from another key agency. Whilst Lisa counteracted this imbalance with her charisma, people skills and hard work, once she had departed, Pam, could not counteract the imbalance in the same way. The partnership came to be seen as merely a mouthpiece of the dominant agency.

It may be helpful to view partnership resources and demands as two sides of a balance (see Figure 4.3). When demands on a partnership are in balance with the resources available, the partnership is usually working well. But when demands outstrip resources, a crisis can ensue, leaving us to consider such questions as:

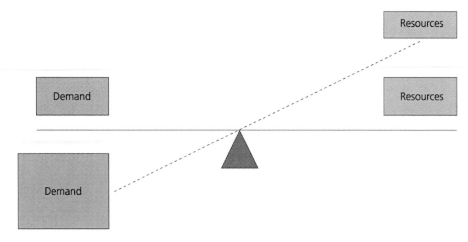

Figure 4.3 The balance between demands and resources.

- How would your partnership react to sudden changes in resources?
- What changes would you need to make in order to deal with this?

Structural faults

Crises are often built into partnerships right at the beginning of their lives, but these only emerge in middle age. These structural faults may have been papered over, but a change in circumstances can bring them to the fore. It is therefore important for every partnership to consider:

- Are there any structural imbalances or deficits in your partnership?
- What changes might you need to make to rectify these?
- If these crises are affecting your partnership, what behaviours and responses can you make to try to deal effectively with them?
- On the other hand, what behaviours or responses will make matters worse?

Helpful responses to crisis

Reaffirming the mandate

A mandate is a command to undertake a particular task which gives those involved the authority to do so. The first and most important grounding for a partnership is that the intended contributors must be given a strong and clear mandate to join and fully participate in the partnership. This mandate may be reflected at all levels of the hierarchy, from central government down to the management structures in local agencies. In times of crisis it seems to be important for this mandate to be regularly re-emphasised and restated, so that the original impetus in working together is renewed.

Thus, in the area of child protection, the mandate to form and sustain interagency partnerships (currently called Area Child Protection Committees or ACPCs) was first issued by Home Office circular in 1950 (Home Office, 1950). Fifty years after this mandate was first issued the government still regularly restates its original instruction to work together: 'The ACPC is an interagency forum for agreeing how the different services and professional groups should cooperate to safeguard children in that area' (DoH, 1999; p33).

At times of crisis, it is not enough merely for government or local agencies to think that a partnership is a good idea: 'organisations are unlikely to take up cooperation with one another simply because someone says it would be a good idea for them to do so' (Weiss, 1981; p29). They must instruct, guide and offer inducements to help those partnerships work. At times of crisis the climate that the partnership operates in may have become difficult: 'The challenge is to create the right climate for collaboration, to recognise the different contributions that participants can make, and to devise organisational arrangements and incentive structures that foster collaborative working' (Hudson, 2000; p254). At times of crises we need to make life inside partnerships possible. Here the main questions that need to be considered are:

- Is the mandate to collaborate clear in your partnership?
- Are there organisational structures and a positive climate that encourage collaboration?
- What can be changed to improve this climate?

Rediscovering the original contract, aims and benefits

One of the difficulties of being in the middle stages of a partnership is that the energy, vision and will to succeed that we frequently experience at the start of the partnership may ebb away in the face of continuing crises or problems. One of the most helpful activities that members can engage in is rediscovering the original contract and aims of the partnership and examining if they are still relevant in the present day (in relationship terms this might be seen as being similar to a process of marriage guidance). We also need to re-examine the roles that individual members have taken on to see if they are still relevant to the partnership and acceptable to the individual member. Collectively and individually the members of the partnership need to work out if the benefits of participating in the partnership outweigh the costs of the partnership work (see Figure 4.2). Ways of doing this are explored in Chapter 6.

Practice Focus 4.5

Things came to a head in the New Initiative partnership when it failed to deliver its annual report and strategy targets. A partnership awayday was organised with an experienced external facilitator. The partnership revisited its original aims and mandate; the loss of Lisa and the vulnerable position of Pam were both acknowledged. The facilitator asked the partnership what needed to change in response to Lisa's departure. The facilitator ended the day by asking each participant to outline why they had agreed to be part of the partnership in the first place and if that commitment was still there. It was crucially important to allow Pam to be part of this reaffirmation exercise.

Rejoining

Confusion of expectations at the start of a partnership or relationship can come back to haunt it in times of crisis: 'The frustration is also due to confusion and conflict over the many unstated assumptions that individuals and organisations take with them to the collaborative arena. Participants are not sure what they are signing themselves up for when they agree to participate and enter into partnership' (Howard, 1994; p21). In the rejoining phase members and agencies involved in the partnership are asked to psychologically rejoin or re-contract themselves to the partnership and to its tasks and aims. The facilitator in Practice Focus 4.5 allowed participants with the experience of middle age to re-evaluate their commitment and to move on into the new stages of the partnership.

Unhelpful responses to crisis

Developing a blame culture: 'We were OK until you came'

When a partnership is faced with a crisis, it is important to achieve a common response to that crisis rather than attempting to lay the blame on a particular member or agency. If a particular member or agency is blamed, this will frequently lead to the crisis becoming more entrenched.

Pretending it's not happening (crisis what crisis?)

Another unhelpful response to a crisis is to pretend that it is not happening. Thus partnership members ignore growing problems until they reach catastrophic proportions, instead of attempting to address the problem in its early stages.

Practice Focus 4.6

Pam found herself increasingly isolated within the partnership. It was obvious to her that the other members were talking about her behind her back. Finally her manager told her that he had received an official complaint about her lack of commitment to the partnership. Pam already felt outnumbered, unable to fill Lisa's shoes and unable to give the partnership enough of her time. Now she was angry and spent all her time covering her back and engaging in critical arguments with those that had complained about her.

Making a mountain out of a molehill (this obstacle is too high for us to climb)

This response is the opposite to pretending a crisis is not happening. It is where one or more partnership members overreact to a problem, claim that the problem is insurmountable and begin to declare that doom is at hand! Partnership members need to take a 'can-do' approach to the obstacles that they meet.

Conflict

Like crises, conflicts in both partnerships and couple relationships are entirely normal. These conflicts may be about internal or external issues, often concerning goals, share of resources, and share of work or interpersonal/interagency processes. Put more simply, these conflicts may be about the share of work and benefits within the partnership and the external goals and direction of the partnership. Gordon (1989) claims that there are six common points of conflict between couples:

- work inside the family
- work outside the family
- sex
- money
- substance use
- extended family relationships

In partnership terms these might translate as work inside the partnership, work outside it, use of partnership resources and relationships with 'home' agencies. Although some people may regard sex and substance abuse as applicable to couple relationships but not to partnerships, we would suggest that this is not actually the case. Interestingly, overindulging in substances has been a frequent cause of partnership conflict, and sexual relationships between key partnership members have been the trigger for bitter conflict between them and/or other partnership members.

Even though conflict is normal, because partnerships rely on their members' ability to collaborate and cooperate on the path to a common goal, it can still threaten partnership survival. Conflict threatens the psychological and organisational agreement to collaborate and therefore may threaten the functioning of the partnership.

Sometimes partnerships are created in areas where interagency conflict is the norm. It is as though by including participants together in a new partnership whole, the hope is that their 'normal' conflict may be avoided. An early example of this was the creation of Area Review Committees (now ACPCs) in 1974. The government noted that interagency conflict impeded child protection work and therefore forced childcare organisations to combine in new protective partnerships. The creation of DATs (drugs action teams) and YOTs (youth offending teams) in the 90s were of similar provenance. However, it is important to realise that this normal conflict may be brought in and acted out within the partnership, often in a covert fashion.

Conflict within partnerships may reflect conflict at other levels in organisations or in society. Thus, Practce Focus 1 in the Introduction to this book deals with a conflict in a development partnership. The conflict in this partnership is a mirror image of the conflict between different government agencies eager to promote their different goals (safer communities, social inclusion for young people and caring for the environment). Partnerships need to acknowledge the existence of these 'higher level' conflicts and try to agree how they shall be dealt with at the partnership level. As with the partnership example in the Introduction, it is usually possible to work out a compromise that allows all participants to achieve some of their goals.

Although all partnerships will experience conflict, some will use the experience to achieve a greater level of collaboration and others may become stuck in the mud of conflict itself. Conflicts, like crises, are frequently an indicator of the need for change within the partnership. Where a partnership becomes stuck, this is often because change is seen to be difficult or impossible. A partnership that engages in constant conflict may eventually cease to function, as all its energy is channelled into the 'civil war' and none to achieving its external goals.

Practice Focus 4.7

The safer situations partnership had enjoyed three very successful years. Relationships had been positive and achievements considerable. However, a minor difference of opinion about a detail in a report led to a bitter, protracted row that seemed to exhaust the positive climate that had been built up. The minor ongoing irritations between partnership members suddenly seemed to take centre stage in all their meetings. Brian was a member of that partnership. For some months he had felt uneasy within the group. When the row about the report surfaced, Brian privately told some members of the partnership that the implications were worse than they had expected and, at the same time, took the author of the report aside and told him that he didn't know what everyone was griping about.

Clearly, then, partnerships need to ask themselves:

- Has the partnership had to deal with serious conflict?
- How did you deal with it?
- Did your partnership get stuck?
- What helped you to become unstuck?

Inter organisational conflict

Separate cultures, languages, tasks, priorities and structures

Interagency conflict is normal in partnerships because members often come from agencies that have created their own unique and separate culture and hold their own perspective on the world:

All practitioners are brought up or accultured in one agency. The practitioner in a particular agency speaks that particular practice language, understands the roles and structure within that practice system and automatically and unconsciously sees the world through that single agency perspective.

Murphy, 2000; p60.

Sometimes these separate cultures lead to conflict and divergence in partnerships. As the chair of one partnership recently stated:

The trickiest bit is trying to hold things together. The different agencies do still have their own flavour. Sometimes we are like icebergs – travelling closely together most of the time, but sometimes in the morning one has drifted off on its own and they are already some distance away.

Ellis, 2000; p2.

When we are building partnerships across agency divides we must remember that consensus and lack of conflict are unusual. Conflict may be the inevitable norm and we need to build up strategies to deal with it positively. Consensus is what comes from the successful management of conflicts, rather than from an absence of such conflicts.

Exploitation or 'colonialism'
This is the organisational attitude that sees a partnership not in terms of what can we achieve together, but how can we exploit partnership resources to benefit our organisation at the expense of others. When combined with a dominance of power of one agency or group it can result in the partnership being taken over and run as a 'colony', with traditional stripping of assets and exploitation of resources.

Interpersonal conflict

Divisive perspectives or behaviours
In just the same way that some individual members of partnerships will undertake helpful roles on behalf of the partnership, some members will bring perspectives and behaviours that foster conflict within the partnership. This may be because the member feels threatened within the partnership and finds reassurance in conflict, or that conflict behaviour is their regular contribution to partnership groups. Many members will see conflict and political infighting between agencies as normal and to be expected. Where this is the case, conflict can be fostered and engendered rather than avoided. The mind set in this case may be not: What can we achieve together?', but 'What can I get out of this partnership for me?' (or 'Do it to them before they do it to you').

Tunnel vision (or single agency thinking)
Although the members of an interagency partnership may feel that they were seeing things from an interagency perspective, it is very easy to slip back into a single agency way of thinking or perceiving:

What keeps us separate, both systemically and professionally, is very powerful and does not diminish over time. Interagency collaboration requires constant attention, re-motivation and energy. It is like building a castle in the sand by the seashore; sometimes the edifice that we create is large, impressive and many-layered, but walls will crumble if left unattended, and also large tidal waves can come and destroy the whole structure.

Murphy, 2000; pp66–7.

In other words, partnerships need constant maintenance work.

Use and/or misuse of power

In terms of partnership working, power can be used both positively and negatively. When it is used positively, this power reinforces cooperative planning and working within the partnership and assists participants in their collaborative endeavours. When it is used negatively, it normally involves one member of the partnership using their power to get their needs met at the expense of the other members, and therefore at the expense of the partnership.

Helpful responses to conflict

In the face of conflict, whether personal or organisational, there are certain responses that can help resolve or mediate the conflict, not least the following.

Common goals

As well as a good understanding of task and process, the most effective 'glue' within partnerships is that the goals of the partnership are held in common. When this is the case, at times of crisis the participants must revisit their original aims or agreements about their common goals. This is not to suggest that a diversity of goals cannot be held within the same partnership, but where those goals come to be seen to be diametrically opposed, and this conflict is not mediated or resolved, the partnership may begin to fail.

Re-establishing an interagency focus

When a partnership comes to be seen to be dominated by the needs or agendas of one powerful agency, it is important to return to an interagency focus and perspective, where all contributions can be valued and the needs of all participants can be at least partially met.

There is a strong parallel here with couple relationships, in so far as there sometimes comes a time when it is necessary to revisit the basis of the relationship and to 'reaffirm the vows'.

Process over task

Where a partnership becomes enmeshed in conflict, it is important to step back temporarily from the task in order to examine what is going wrong with the process. In the same way, if the partnership has become very influenced by participants who indulge in divisive behaviours, it is most important to bring back to the fore those members who have inclusion, compromise and collaboration as part of their role within the partnership. These members will frequently have group process skills and will push a collaborative agenda within the partnership:

> These skills include the ability to influence how the task is seen, to translate the reality of single agency perspectives to other practitioner groups, and to act as conciliator, mediator and diplomat in the face of interagency conflict or dispute.
>
> Murphy, 2000; pp65–6.

Mediation

In any kind of partnership or relationship conflict, it is often the subjective, perceived meaning behind the behaviour, rather than the objective behaviour itself that we experience as destructive. The common mediation technique of exploring the meaning behind the behaviour is often useful in moving partnerships in conflict to a different stage.

Unhelpful responses to conflict

Ganging up: 'It's all your fault'

Although we live in a society that seems to enjoy finding out who is to blame, this blaming behaviour tends not to be helpful in partnerships. The very process of blame, vilification and scapegoating gives negative messages to other participants, leaving them anxious and unwilling to take risks:

> Although some interagency lessons can be learned from this allocation of blame, in the long term, the damage caused to practitioners and systems by such negative critical focus, is profound. The tendency to blame frequently leaves individuals and agencies in a state of extreme stress and low morale, which in turn negatively affects their ability to work in a positive interagency way.

Murphy, 2000; p66.

The development of a culture of blame is therefore something to be avoided wherever possible.

Pretending it's not there

Often at the early stages of conflict, partnership members will pretend that the conflict is not taking place. This is done in the hope that it will 'blow over'. Unfortunately, some conflicts do not blow over on their own, and partnership will become an increasingly uncomfortable and unproductive place to be if the tendency to avoid 'biting the bullet' is allowed to predominate.

Conclusion

As we have seen in this chapter, the middle stages or maturity of partnerships have their own difficult processes to contend with. Using examples of crisis and conflict, we have explored the different ways that partnerships can respond to these problems of middle age, suggesting that caring within the partnership may assist in overcoming these inevitable difficulties. The questions that follow are designed to help your partnership understand, and to deal with, the 'keeping going' stage:

- What can crisis and conflict in the middle stages of partnership be seen as?
- What are the common causes of crisis?
- What helpful responses to crisis can the partnership employ?
- What unhelpful responses might the partnership get stuck in?
- What are the common causes of conflict at this stage of partnership?
- What helpful responses to conflict can the partnership employ?
- What unhelpful responses might the partnership get stuck in?
- Why should we strive to look after ourselves and our colleagues within our partnership work?

Chapter 5

Moving On: Transition, Transformation and Termination

Introduction

Relationships end, even though, at the beginning, we may pretend that this will never happen. It is exactly the same with partnerships. When we set out along the partnership road, endings could not be further from our minds. The pain, conflict and thoughts of failure that are associated with endings often lead us to deny its very possibility. When we find ourselves in the middle of endings we are frequently beset by all kinds of unhelpful emotions. In Chapter 3 we looked at the possibilities and pitfalls for making partnerships more structured; in this chapter we explore what happens to partnerships when they come to an end.

What's the point of learning about endings?

As we shall note below, there are numerous variations in the ways to end a partnership. But why write about them? Isn't such time as we have for exploring ideas and developing partnership skills better spent learning about building them up rather then breaking them down? And when breakdown happens, isn't it all just chaotic anyway? Isn't it better just to move on and quickly be done with it? As one of the present authors put it:

> Drafting the chapter on endings had to be done right at the time when a partnership project I had been working on for about two years had its public launch. The last thing I wanted to think through was what happens when partnerships come to an end – not least because we inevitably had quite enough struggles and challenges getting things started in the first place.

But another partner shed a different light on the matter: 'Are you telling me that no-one should ever get divorced?' Suddenly it seemed selfish to make no effort to think through and try to share what happens when partnerships break down.

We have to be very wary of the tendency to neglect endings, as if to assume that they will somehow sort themselves out. As Thompson (2002) argues, a failure to pay attention to the subtleties involved in ensuring positive endings can lead to a number of problems, not least the undoing of much of the good work that has been done prior to the ending. It also has to be recognised that effectively managing the conclusion of a project is a highly skilled activity. It involves not only the 'people' skills involved in managing the relationships involved, but also the planning and management skills involved in making sure that the necessary loose ends are tied up, lessons are learned for future reference, strengths are identified and built on, future working relationships are safeguarded, benefits of the partnership are recognised, celebrated and maximised, and the job satisfaction that motivates us to keep going is enjoyed and appreciated.

Even where partnerships end in acrimony and failure, there is still much to be gained from maximising those benefits which have accrued, learning any lessons and using the experience as a foundation for future successful work. It is therefore important to recognise that there is something positive to be gained from any ending, regardless of the circumstances. This is a point to which we shall return in Chapter 6 where we explore issues of evaluation.

Breakdown and its aftermath in human relationships have been widely written about and discussed. It is often observed that the pain of breakdown is lessened, for partners and children, if the process is considered and managed (Hyden, 2001). Of course, moving on is not all about pain and remorse. As in many divorces, an ending of one thing is often a new beginning of something else. Indeed, the ending may be the very thing that makes a fresh start possible.

At the end of our partnership, do we want to experience bitter conflictual separations that leave us absorbed in endless recriminations, or do we wish to experience considered annulments that leave us ready to carry on looking after the children and joining other partnerships? How can we manage the process to make it less painful than it might be if we just let it run its course and bury our heads in the sand?

Having our eyes wide open at this difficult time may help us to recognise what is happening and help us and our partners to cope better. If we refuse to understand partnership breakdown, how can we hope to try to help clients who have come to value or depend on what the partnership has been providing? With this in mind, we have tried to write this chapter in a way that will help any of you who are involved in endings to look forward positively to the opportunities, challenges and new partnerships that may lie ahead.

Within this fine balance of optimism and realism, in this chapter we explore:

- What lies behind the desire to move on and what types of ending we may need to deal with.
- The psychological processes of ending for ourselves and others.
- Particular aspects of partnership that we will need to manage during any kind of ending.
- The ceremonies of ending.

Each theme could be a book in itself. However, rather than describe easy, guided routes along well-trodden paths, we try to help you to think about your options, how you can explore and map them, and the importance of thinking and adapting as you go – not just relying on established routes and techniques – and thereby developing the skills of partnership that are relevant in this context.

Different routes to endings

In what circumstances might endings happen? One day, instead of deciding to work with your partners in a more structured way, one of the partners may want to move out of the partnership:

> *Local authorities and health bodies will have the right to withdraw from voluntary care trusts, health minister John Hutton has announced. He agreed to amend the Health and Social Care Bill . . . to include a clause allowing either party to end an arrangement at 'the earliest time practicable.'*
> Community Care, 15–21 Feb, 2001; p3.

'We need to talk . . .' These dreaded words often mean not only that we may not have been talking enough to this point, but also that talk from now on will be about bringing the relationship to an end. One day the resources that a partnership needs (funding, energy, enthusiasm and so on) may just run out; and with that, the partnership has to be brought to an end, often despite the wishes of those involved.

Sometimes we may want to get out of a partnership, but can only do so if we leave our current post. Members of some government-mandated partnerships (for example, Area Child Protection Committees) have to stay together despite personal preferences. In some partnerships participants are held by less formal, but perhaps equally binding partnership pressures.

Practice Focus 5.1

When Sue volunteered to help the young people's project, she thought she knew what she was letting herself in for. It was all carefully explained and she took what she heard at face value. Now she felt like a young mother who told her how she started out doing bar work, went along when Tuesdays became topless and started lap-dancing to get a friend out of a pickle. But, despite Sue's anger at herself and her partners over how she had let herself be manipulated into taking on too much, and despite the incredible stresses that she had to deal with as a result, she didn't want to stop now – like that young mother – because of the kids.

Others may feel trapped by partnership conditions imposed by major stakeholders. For example, much Single Regeneration Budget (SRB) and Lottery funding requires grant recipients to prove that they are working in partnership before resources are allocated.

As these examples illustrate, there are many different ways of reaching an ending. The ending itself may be of:

- an entire partnership
- parts of a partnership
- your role in a partnership, that will carry on after you have left.

The ending may be one that has been coming for a long time and has been anticipated (many City Challenge or SRB partnerships will come under this category). The ending may have been planned because the piece of work has come to an end. If the partnership has been set up for one specific purpose, this goal may have been achieved. Some partnerships, however, end suddenly because of a change in external factors (a change of legislation, government, funding and so on) or because of a change of internal factors (for example, a sudden crisis or conflict within the partnership).

But, as we noted in Chapter 3 on tying the knot, when we are considering 'moving on' we again need to look at:

- Managing yourself so that you can successfully represent your organisation within the partnership while it is going through such a major change. One way of putting it would be: 'No one said divorce was going to be easy. That's why you need my services as a lawyer, certainly until the marriage is formally over and quite possibly afterwards.'
- Minimising the pain of such changes while you consider, decide on and act on them: 'No-one said divorce was going to be easy. That's why I am here to help you as a counsellor.'

In the process of helping you in this way, we hope also to illustrate the nature and outcomes of 'moving on' in such a way as to help you decide whether you want to do so. Although the visions of outcomes may be exactly the opposite to those in 'tying the knot', the processes and tasks involved in working towards each vision will nevertheless have many similarities.

Given those similarities in the processes and tasks between tying the knot and moving on, let us now look at whether the framework used in that chapter can be used here as well. The chapter looked at:

1. *Making a proposal.* The reasons why you or your partners might want to make a change in some way.
2. *Getting cold feet.* The anxieties that may be aired about possible pitfalls and dangers.
3. *Options.* A look at the range of changes that is available.
4. *Thinking about your options.* An analysis of the process of deciding whether or not to make a change.
5. *Negotiating it.*
6. *Doing it/acting on it.* Exploring and mapping what happens next.
7. *Celebrating it.*
8. *Sustaining it.* Living with it and getting out of it.
9. *Looking after yourself.* Some of the potential effects on you as an employee during this stage of partnership work.

You may find this model of process useful in exploring endings but, given that it was designed for a different purpose, there will inevitably be some limitations to its use in this context.

Change: assimilation and accommodation

The child development theorist, Jean Piaget describes two different processes involved in children growing up and learning how to adapt to the changes they experience:

- *Assimilation.* Change that can be assimilated within existing ways of looking at the world (what are known as 'schemata', or frameworks of understanding).
- *Accommodation.* Change that requires new ways of looking at the world through the development of new schemata. (See Piaget and Inhelder, 1966).

In the same way, partnerships and partnership workers will need to address:

- *Assimilation.* Change that can be assimilated within an ongoing partnership.
- *Accommodation.* Change that forces the partnership to break down or alter radically.

Assimilation has been dealt with in Chapter 4 on *Keeping Going*, where we looked at some of the things that can happen when a partner leaves or when a new one arrives. This chapter looks at changes that require some form of accommodation or dissolution.

The desire to move on: 'We gotta get out of this place'

What might lie behind a desire to get out of a partnership? This line from the song by The Animals (1961) is one that has probably struck a chord in all of us at one time or another. Perhaps such an impulse to move on is because:

- You despair of ever getting yourself out of the difficult and painful state of constant change that characterises partnership: 'I just can't take it any more!'
- In spite of all difficulties, the job you set out to do is done: 'It's great. The kids have grown up and can stand on their own feet. I can live my own life again' can be equated with 'The community learning centre has its own management team and board of trustees now, and has become financially self-sustaining.'
- The circumstances of one partner have changed: 'Darling! The business is being restructured. I've got to move away . . . (pause) we'll stay in touch somehow.'
- An external factor, such as legislation, has changed: 'It was wrong of us to try to force you to marry that (wo)man. We've found someone much better for you! All change!'
- Your partner doesn't want you any more: 'Please. I've had enough of your awful behaviour. Just leave. Now.'

Each different way of ending brings its own attendant issues. In this series of snapshots we have seen a range of issues. They include:

- *Personal issues*: stress; burnout; frustration; yearning.
- *Organisational issues*: anger; failure; scandal; the demand for change; conflict; success.
- *External issues*: funding; policy; clients' requirements; the unexpected: a crisis or disaster.

How can we make sense of how these might come together?

Even though breaking up may be necessary or unavoidable, it is often, in the words of the song, 'hard to do'. Therefore, you should weigh very carefully whether it is going to be of help to you, your organisation, and your partners and, above all, your clients before you take this course. For this process to be as painless as possible, it is essential that you and your organisation have your eyes open, think clearly and defend the values that underpin the service that you aim to provide during the separation and afterwards.

The psychological processes of ending for ourselves and others

In Chapter 3 we focused on the psychological issues of tying the knot. In this chapter it seems even more important to talk about these processes. This is because, at a time of breakdown, emotions will very probably be running high and can easily become a dominant factor in charting the partnership's course. We also need to state the obvious, which is that different parts of a partnership might be experiencing different thought processes and feelings at the same time.

What are these emotions?

Those that may be causing you and your partners to begin thinking about breaking up may well include: isolation, bitterness, frustration, anger, jealousy and weariness. Sometimes these emotions will relate to your partners. Sometimes they will relate to people and organisations outside the partnership that are causing your work together to come to an end. Sometimes they may even come from other parts of your life that are impinging on your partnership commitments. By the time the breakdown is complete, these emotions may well be supplemented by: loss, grief, desire for vengeance, loneliness and yearning.

Relationships with ex-partners

Where can we put these emotions? Who can we give them to? Is it better to seek an outside recipient (they are to blame!) or is it better to vent these feelings within the partnership itself? Often former participants will have to carry on having dealings with the partners long after the partnership breaks down. The key to these future relationships may lie in who is seen to be to blame for the breakdown (whether that blame is held *internally* or *externally*).

Practice Focus 5.2

The Connaught Square neighbourhood project was made up of a committed number of partnership members whose aim was to improve their local neighbourhood. The partnership was totally funded by the local authority. A change of political administration led to withdrawal of funding. Partnership members were furious with elected members, and many meetings and letters of protest were sent to the council and to MPs. However, as all the blame for the partnership ending was allocated to external factors, the positive relationship between the members of the partnership was maintained – so much so that, one year later, the partnership was reformed with support from an alternative funding source.

But if the 'blame' for ending lies with one or more of the partnership members, positive relationships after breakdown are more difficult to achieve. As in a couple relationship breakdown, bitter arguments can continue, long after the ending, concerning who was to blame for that breakdown. Recriminations can so easily become the order of the day.

This is the key to future relationships with ex-partners. How much are they to blame for the breakdown or how much blame can be located elsewhere? When blame is held internally the future relationships between ex-partners can be difficult, and fraught with unresolved conflict.

Where they can be attributed to external factors future relationships can be much easier.

However, the whole question of 'blame' needs to be handled very carefully and sensitively. If not, we can easily produce a vicious circle in which bad feelings may become hostile feelings and may, in turn, lead to further recriminations.

Those left behind

If this is how the participants in partnership are feeling on ending, then what are the feelings of the recipients of that partnership work going to be? And how much do you have to deal with them? As with divorce and relationship breakdown, it is easy to become totally absorbed in adult/partner business and ignore the separate, different feelings of the children/recipients. As a minimum the recipients need to be offered the following:

- A true account of why the partnership is coming to an end.
- Details of where they can send their perceptions on this ending.
- Information about who will be continuing to provide a service (if anyone).
- Information about alternative provision of similar services.
- Inclusion in the ceremonies of ending (see below).

Managing the breakdown processes: 'There must be some kind of way out of here'

This declaration, made by 'the joker to the thief' in Bob Dylan's 'All Along the Watchtower', is about managing yourself and others in this context. This is going to be difficult and the temptation to run away will be strong. This can be manifest in the desire to:

- Use your abilities on something constructive, rather than destructive.
- Find new opportunities, income and/or security.
- Get rid of all the difficult and rather negative feelings.
- Get out first and not to be the last one left, having to 'put the lights out' on the partnership.

But, if we look at breakdowns in couple relationships, there are plenty of reminders that, although the partnership may be coming to an end, responsibilities continue and, even when emotions are raw, we need to carry on thinking about our responsibilities to ourselves, our partners, clients and colleagues in our 'home' organisations.

We also need to ask: How can we chart a course of action that lets us honour these responsibilities at such a difficult time? We need to ask ourselves:

- What is the timeframe?
- Do we have to dispose of any assets?
- Who do we have to negotiate with?
- Who do we have to tell?
- What records need to be kept?
- Who may need help as a result of the breakdown?
- What resources do we have to help us in this process (money, advice, guidance)?

As Pledger (2001) states:

> There is a wealth of information, advice and support out there when you want to start up a new organisation, but when it comes to winding up, often as not it's just one or two people who are left holding the baby as it were. There isn't much support available if you want to make sure that all the loose ends are tied up and the organisation is wound up properly.
>
> p10.

The author goes on to stress the value and importance of accountants and the Charity Commission Helpline (0870 333 0123). She argues that:

> . . . for the most part winding up is the opposite of starting up and pretty much a common sense process. But when you're actually in the situation it can be a bit difficult to see your way and may be even a little daunting, so we've made a list of bullet points of the things that you need to remember to do.
>
> p10.

Pledger's list is worthy of our consideration:

- The first thing, of course, is to make sure that you have explored all the options. Do you really have to wind up? Is that the right thing to do? Are there no better alternatives? You may find it helpful to talk this through with someone outside your organisation.

- Next there has to be a decision to wind up from the management committee. Usually this will also have to be ratified by a general meeting of all your members. Your constitution will be a useful guide for you on this.

- After this, you should make sure that all your organisation's debts and liabilities are settled. If this is one of the reasons why you are winding up (for example, you have no money left or you are in financial difficulty), then you need some help. You may wish to speak to your accountant about this, and this is certainly something that we would recommend.

- Once you have your finances in order and have paid off all your debts and so on, you need to find out what property or money your group has left. Some constitutions say that resources that are left over should be given to a similar kind of charity or charitable organisation.

- Once you have done all these things you need to tell people you are winding up. This includes other groups you work with, your volunteers, service users and, of course, if you are registered, you need to inform the Charity Commission.

- If you are a registered charity, you will need to produce a set of final accounts. Even if you are not a registered charity, we would argue that it is a good idea to do this anyway, and give your members and management committee a final set of accounts to show what has happened to any leftover monies.

Practice Focus 5.3

When the time came to wind up the partnership, the key players involved did not initially appreciate how much work was involved or how many tasks needed to be done. It brought home to them how complex a job it is to bring a partnership to a close. It was not simply a case of saying goodbye and going their separate ways. 'We will have to set up a partnership to manage the winding down of this one', joked one of the partners. All involved realised from this experience that it is no simple matter to bring a partnership to a close, and they accepted that they had not given this enough consideration in their planning. The positive thing, though, was that, although they had learned the hard way, they *had* learned the lesson, and each of them would be much more tuned in to the need to plan and manage endings effectively in any future partnership ventures they may be involved with.

There is a range of other things that you will need to do, some of them quite simple and others more complex:

- redirecting any mail
- cancelling any subscriptions and direct debits
- closing down utility supplies
- releasing employees
- and so on

Neither the importance nor the potentially time-consuming nature of all these things should be underestimated. Some of them may be easier because you are in a partnership. For example, your property and employees may always have been linked to individual organisations rather than the partnership. But some may be complex, especially if one of the reasons for partnership breakdown was internal conflict or difficulty in communication and/or decision-making.

The rituals of ending

Within our society we are very good at marking the beginning of new life stages or processes. So our baptisms, weddings, coming of age celebrations and so on are all well attended, enjoyed and esteemed. Our initial reaction might be to believe that we are less good at celebrating our endings, but in some prescribed situations we will all participate in and benefit from ending ceremonies. These ending ceremonies include leaving work or retirement, end of a production or performance and, of course, end-of-life funerals. Often these ceremonies offer us a chance to come together, to mourn, to talk about the past and the future and to reassure ourselves about the world. Rituals play an important part in helping us to sustain 'ontological security', to feel rooted in our lifeworlds, often at times when major changes can undermine our sense of who we are and where we fit into the world.

Practice Focus 5.4

Denise had been involved in two largely unconnected partnerships for quite some time but, by sheer coincidence, they both came to an end in the same month. She was surprised by the major impact this had on her. She felt as though she had lost someone and was grieving. This was a very powerful feeling, and was quite disabling for a while, even though she felt that it was 'silly' to have such feelings and tried to put them to one side.

The impact on her was so great that she spent a lot of time thinking back over her partnership experiences and the varied feelings they had evoked in her. One thing she realised from this period of reflection was that, while she had put immense efforts into both partnerships and had got a lot out of both of them, they had been very different in how they ended. One had involved a formal celebration of the partnership as it came to a close, in which the successes were identified and affirmed. The other, however, although it had been equally successful, had no such formal acknowledgement of its achievements, and this left a sense of emptiness and disappointment, something which reinforced Denise's feelings of grief.

What lessons can we learn from these ending ceremonies and what may we transfer into the partnership arena to make our endings more positive? The following ideas are just some of the important ones to consider:

- It is better to have a ceremony than not to have one. Without some form of ceremony to 'mark' the occasion, the positives of the occasion may not be fully appreciated, and you may also miss the opportunity to cement working relationships for the benefit of future partnerships or other forms of collaboration.

- It is better to invite a wide number of members and recipients of partnership services. Just as it is now commonly accepted that it is a mistake not to include the children at a family funeral, we should be able to see that not including certain people may lead to problems, tensions and resentment that may stand in the way of future joint work or may even undermine the benefits of what has been achieved by the partnership.

- A good ceremony allows participants to remember and value the good things that have been experienced. Even a partnership that has major problems and may have been a significant disappointment in a number of ways, is still likely to have had some positives – if only the lessons that can be learned from the negative experiences.

- A good ceremony allows participants to mourn the passing of those things. Endings involve a degree of loss and perhaps grief, so rituals can be very helpful in helping people come to terms with the losses involved (Moss, 2002).

- More controversially, if it can be accomplished safely, a ceremony might allow the discussion of the more negative parts of the partnership. (Be careful with this one – in the song, *Finnegan's Wake*, the funeral goers start a riot because of the long-held disagreements about the departed one.)

  Ending ceremonies can help us resolve issues in our heads and hearts, they can help us make a closer bond with ex-partners that increases the likelihood of successful future partnership work. Of course, they should not be used as an opportunity to replay old partnership conflicts, as that is likely to *decrease* the chances of successful future collaborations, rather than increase them.

Conclusion

Endings are one of the most difficult stages of any partnership. This chapter has offered some ideas for how to negotiate the ending stage positively. Our advice can perhaps be summed up as follows:

- Keep your eyes open and don't run – seeing it through will be better in the long term. It will also help you decide whether 'ending it' is what you want to do.

- Understand the different reasons behind and types of endings – your response will have to 'fit' the circumstances that you find yourself in.

- The psychological processes and feelings of partnerships can be powerful – often conflictual and negative. These feelings can be affected by who is seen to be to 'blame'. If these feelings can be expressed without bitter conflict, it is good to express them in order to move on.

Because of the difficulty of endings, there is a tendency to ignore them or get them over as soon as possible. Ending processes are as complex and difficult to manage as any other around partnership, but a good ending confirms the work that has already been done and frees partners to fully join new partnerships. It is important to try to manage these endings effectively so that ex-partners and service users are included, and future partnerships remain possible.

We have emphasised that ending a partnership should involve:

- Learning from the experience (building on the positives and avoiding the mistakes and the negatives) so that we can be better equipped for partnership in future.

- Celebrating that experience (saluting the positives and leaving behind the negatives).

These are both complex issues that merit closer attention, which is why they reappear in Chapter 6, where they are considered in more depth. It is therefore to these that we now turn.

Chapter 6

In Praise of Partnership

Introduction: do we value our partnerships?

In Chapters 3 and 5 we considered two options for major change in partnerships. In one direction we explored tying the knot (Chapter 3), with a view to making a partnership into a more formal, structured and binding arrangement. In the other direction we explored moving on (Chapter 5), either by leaving a partnership or breaking it up completely.

Both options offered possibilities for securing a range of benefits for you, your partners and your clients. But neither was shown to be an easy path, and the possible pitfalls were numerous. Neither was found to be a clear-cut panacea for any ills that a partnership might be suffering, nor for any ills that you might personally experience within that partnership. So, while you and your partners might well have occasion to tie the knot or move on, you might equally decide that keeping going in your current partnership is the right choice for you, despite the stresses and strains that had made you consider a major change in the first place.

In this book we have already offered insights into how partnership can be less painful than it might be. Can we now, for those who elect to keep going in this way – and for those who have no choice – add a new sense of what partnership is good for? Can we find a way, even, to speak up in praise of partnership? Can we do this in a way that makes sense – not just to those looking at a partnership from the outside (policy makers and funders, for example) but also to those agencies and clients inside it?

This chapter tries to help us to value partnership. Much has been written on the evaluation of the phenomenon of partnership in general and specific partnerships in particular. Given that the evaluation of partnership working involves money, politicians and intellectuals, it is bound to be disputed territory! So perhaps we won't convince everyone, but we hope that, having come this far in our partnership between authors and readers, you will want to keep going and see if what we have learned from others can help you here too.

Partners make up their own minds

Over recent years, working in partnership has often been presented by politicians and policy makers as an unquestioned good thing. Its benefits to society would indeed seem to be obvious. But this book has been written in response to the pressures and demands on those who are asked and sometimes ordered to work in partnership – pressures sometimes so strong that, in their resulting views, partnership is far from obviously beneficial. Acknowledging such concerns, in this chapter we explore ways in which partners can make up their own minds about what their partnership is good at, and where it might do better. Specifically, we:

- Set the context for such a 'personal' evaluation.
- Establish that each of us should expect our voice to be heard in any wider evaluation of a partnership in which we are working.

- Get you started in thinking about some of the positive and negative experiences of working in your partnership.
- Stress that, when talking about what is good, and not so good about a partnership for you, you must be prepared to speak up in ways that your partners can comprehend and absorb.
- Stress, in turn, that our partners have these same rights and responsibilities.
- Suggest how you can set up a cross-partnership evaluation, negotiate partners' roles, and work together to make change.
- Explore how you can negotiate the content of an evaluation with your partners, both your achievements and how they are achieved.
- Propose celebrating partnership, and ask how best to do that.

Just as a couple relationship is likely to benefit from time devoted to reflecting on the benefits of the relationship (and appreciating what each partner gains from it and how it can perhaps be improved), partnerships can similarly benefit from reflection on what works well and should be built on, and what does not work so well and should be changed. Partnerships of any kind, whether a couple relationship or an interorganisational or inter-professional partnership, can benefit from 'maintenance' – time spent on reviewing the situation and making sure that the channels of communication remain open. Couples can have difficulties if they start to take each other for granted; partnerships too can suffer if they do not revisit the basis of their collaboration and remind themselves of the value of what they are doing.

Partnership options: complex choices

When we were considering tying the knot with our partners, as a way of creating a more formal structure for operations and decision making, we considered that 'having cold feet' was to be expected. Reasons for this might include the possibilities that:

- Tying the knot might actually signal the end of the benefits of working together. For example, the opportunity of small organisations to sit at the same table with some of the bigger ones, and to express their views and values, might be lost – perhaps along with other opportunities and freedoms.
- A bigger, more formal structure might become less (rather than more) efficient and hard to adapt at a later date.
- Once a bigger, possibly stronger organisation was established, critics might have a bigger target to aim at.
- Clients might not notice the difference and be left wondering what the knot-tying fuss was all about.
- As in a couple relationship, the arguments might not end.

When examining the processes of tying the knot, we saw how none of these were irrational anxieties. We acknowledged that several partnerships might quite appropriately choose to organise more formally, either their entire partnership, or selected projects and processes within them. But we concluded that such major and binding change could not be recommended for all partnerships, and should be undertaken lightly by none.

When, alternatively, we were thinking about moving on – leaving or breaking up the partnership – we also had cold feet because of the following:

- Anger and frustration with partners might be replaced by nothing more than bitterness and a desire for revenge.
- Loss of current partners might just precipitate a search for new ones.
- Clients might be left wondering more than ever why organisations all purporting to serve them cannot work effectively together.
- Politicians and funding agencies might adopt a similar view and make their resources harder to obtain.

Again we concluded that there will be occasions when moving on is the right choice, or even inescapable. There will be times too when projects and processes that you have set up within a partnership come to an end of their useful lives, while the partnership itself carries on. But we were left reflecting that 'breaking up is hard to do': the complex dynamics of splitting up and the administrative organisation of divorce can be difficult and demanding.

If, for such reasons, neither of these choices seems right, your pursuit of the third option, keeping going in an existing partnership, may well be helped by trying to clarify in your mind how the partnership is helping you, and how it might not be, and how to make it better.

Of course, such an evaluation is not easy. So we start with the need to accept that partnerships are complicated. For most of us, partnerships between just two people are complicated. When the people in a partnership are representatives of organisations situated outside the partnership, the complexity increases. So too when the number of partners rises. Furthermore, some partners may be involved in other partnerships. While some people in the partnership leave, others arrive.

All this can be difficult to keep straight. So, trying to be clear about the value of a partnership will probably be complicated too, even when you are just trying to make your own mind up about something rather than trying to convince someone else. But, it is not impossible and, if done with care, can make a real difference in helping you – and your partners – achieve your goals.

Is anyone listening?

It is nevertheless true that many of us duck out of the task of trying to evaluate a partnership. Beyond this sense that it is too complicated, there is also a strong feeling that our partners do not listen, and that there is therefore no point. The temptation can be strong to spend our time instead compiling evidence to justify such fears that our views do not count: that we are partnership victims rather than partnership participants. Indeed, such fears may not be groundless. If there are problems in how you work together, there are very probably going to be difficulties in how you evaluate your work together.

If an evaluation is being done to secure funding, isn't there going to be competition for resources? If it is being done to secure public recognition, are some agencies going to present themselves more positively than they present their partners? Do we need to be on the lookout for an agency getting us into trouble as an outcome of trying to exonerate them from blame? Are judgements being made by one or more powerful agencies while others are left out? If an external evaluator is involved, how do we make sure that they do more than listen to the loudest and most powerful? These are big questions, and they can be a powerful force for taking the easy way out. We evade the tasks of evaluation in favour of lobbying or even protesting. A blame culture can seem attractive compared with one where we accept responsibility and ownership.

Inclusive evaluation

An equally powerful argument, when a partnership is being evaluated, may therefore be needed for encouraging us to think carefully, to speak up and persuade others to listen. A good one can be found in Gersh Subhra's paper, 'Reclaiming the Evaluation Agenda' (Subhra, 2001). It is a useful summary of the development of methods of evaluation, especially for readers who may not be experts in this area, and gives all of us – expert and non-expert alike – the encouragement to participate. It also seems very relevant. Although he is writing about community work with young people, there is a strong resonance in his views with those expressed by partnership workers when they feel as though they are serving funding agencies at the expense of clients, or submerged beneath other agencies' values and agendas.

Amongst his goals are the creation of opportunities for workers to ensure that:

- Their value base, philosophy and methods of working are adequately incorporated in any evaluation of their work.

- They can demonstrate the impact and value of the work that they are doing – and not leave it to funders and managers who may only make their own case.

- They thereby 'reclaim' the evaluation agenda.

Before we return to trying to help clarify in your mind how a partnership is helping you, and how it might not be, we want to share with you and try to learn from Subhra's rationale and recommendations that make his goals achievable.

Representative evaluation

Alongside his desire to ensure that evaluation is inclusive, Subhra goes on to recommend that it should also be representative. He suggests that an overemphasis on 'quantitative and mechanistic performance indicators, inputs, outputs and outcomes' may 'exclude the subjective dynamics of communities, interpersonal relations and aspirations' and result in an 'incomplete analysis' (p71). Rather, citing Russell (1998), he recommends that evaluations should include:

- Qualitative data (narratives, stories, case studies and so on).
- A belief in multiple realities.
- Valuing subjective perspectives.
- Seeing understanding as something different from measurement.
- Embracing paradox and acknowledging uncertainties and ambiguities.
- Acknowledging that values inevitably impinge on the evaluative process. (p72)

Can those of us who are striving to make sense of working in partnership learn from this?

Practice Focus 6.1

Kathleen attended a conference on evidence-based practice and, while she was not entirely convinced by the arguments being put forward in favour of it, she did find it a stimulating and thought-provoking conference. In particular, she came away with a strong commitment to the importance of evaluation. She gave a lot of thought to how she could not only evaluate her own work within her own agency, but also put evaluation on the agenda of the partnerships she was involved with. However, she realised that this was going to be a very complex task, given the differing perspectives and interests of the various stakeholders. She realised that evaluating partnership work was going to be a big challenge, but one that she and her partners should not shirk.

Are partnerships like communities?

Subhra is, of course, writing about the evaluation of community work, in particular that involving young people. It is perhaps pushing things too far in our already extended analogy between partnerships and couple relationships to dwell extensively on the nature of relationships in communities, and thereby learn what partnerships between multiple agencies (communities of agencies, if you like) can learn from community workers about evaluation.

But we can note at least some parallels between social communities and partnerships of agencies. In both there is:

- complexity of agents, networks and communication
- diversity of members and what they represent
- the possibility of power and resource imbalances
- many possible routes to either conflict or consensus.

The parallel has obvious limits. There are differences of scale in size, complexity and diversity. Work partnerships are brought together for some reasonably clear purpose, or at least with the hope of defining one, whereas to ascribe this to postmodern communities would be impossible.

But, when we explore further issues of 'purpose', this distinction blurs. Like communities, partnerships can sometimes be thrown together by accident. As in communities, the search for a high level of shared purpose in partnership, can be emotionally intense, but it can equally end up excluding or devaluing some members. Indeed, the search in partnerships for something akin to the founding myths of communities may not be fruitless. And, while many communities in today's post-modern and globalised world can seem so fractured that they lack any kind of coherent purpose, their members will usually have some shared aspirations – for example, for safety, health, shelter, long life, nourishment and the opportunity to pursue a good life.

Having thus raised at least the possibility of learning about partnerships at work by studying the ideas and practices of those who work in communities, we recommend Subhra's work as a concise and well-founded presentation of useful ideas that are presented in a friendly format. We have cited, in the 'Guide to further study' section at the end of the book, his complete references: initially those that he uses to chart the historic and conceptual development of evaluation and then those that may help in developing further his recommendations for action, so that those of you who may not have had a chance to read them can develop your own ideas.

'Reclaiming the evaluation agenda'

At the heart of Subhra's work is a framework which he calls 'a strategy for reclaiming the evaluation agenda'. Its purpose is to help not just 'the controlling sponsors' but also 'the learning practitioner' (citing Armstrong and Key, 1979; p73). Each can use it to promote both accountability to external stakeholders and learning and development within the organisation. These goals seem of obvious value to anyone who wants to improve their relationships with other groups and organisations, nurture their own and colleagues' personal development and improve the services that they aim to provide together. We contend that they are therefore of relevance to those working in partnerships.

To achieve these goals Subhra suggests that an effective evaluation should include a range of components, several of which are set out in the box below (see Subhra, 2001; pp73–7). We have added our comments in brackets to help you explore his ideas in the context of partnership working. We recommend that you ask yourself how each may be of help when you deliberate how to evaluate a partnership, whether on your own or with your partners. Some ideas may be of more immediate relevance to you than others, but all are probably worth giving reasonably careful thought.

Subhra's framework for reclaiming the evaluation agenda

1. Recognition that:

- 'There are different perspectives, depending on . . . the type of agency that is carrying out the work'

- 'The level of capacity and resourcing needed to carry out effective evaluation' should be recognised as 'a key part of negotiation with funders [and partners] . . . at the outset.'

2. The need to question whether there can 'be greater involvement of the staff team, management committee, other volunteers and community members' (to which we would add partners) in the evaluation.

3. A proposal for the integration of evaluation that 'assesses how closely evaluation priorities and activities integrate into the various functions of an organisation's [partnership's] routine operations . . . [These might include] planning, policy making, recruitment and selection, supervision and appraisal systems, equal opportunities policies and systems, staff development and training, public relations, fund-raising strategies and so on.' Each, Subhra argues, 'offer opportunities for evaluation to feature significantly and an audit may uncover some useful ways in which the profile of evaluation could be raised.'

4. A clear sense of purpose about what anyone wants evaluation information for:

- Is it, for instance, to try and calculate value for money?

- Is it for the sponsors – or partners – public relations purposes?

- Is it to encourage your agency to learn and develop clarity about the work being undertaken?

- Is it just an administrative exercise that allows the agency to demonstrate accountability to the funder?

- Have they resorted to a relatively mechanistic evaluation framework because they are unfamiliar with the type of qualitative data to ask for?

5. A commitment to include 'the intangible aspects of . . . [partnership] work' an example of which 'could be the substantial amount of time that some agencies and workers have to spend in building up relationships of trust with, say, young people' or other clients, or volunteers, or indeed, partners.

6. A reminder that, whereas evaluation is commonly regarded as an analysis of the degree of progress towards the original project objectives, such objectives are neither fixed nor limited in number. They are often augmented on either a formal or informal basis by stakeholders involved in funding or carrying out the work: 'This, in essence, represents the fluidity of [partnership] work that is constantly and cyclically involved in . . . assessing needs . . . re-negotiating how groups respond to policy changes . . . having to re-prioritise because of the changes in the composition and skills capacity of the community groups [partners] . . . dealing with conflicts . . . responding to unforeseen funding opportunities.'

7. The argument that a partnership initiative that does not generate new objectives is 'perhaps being inflexible and dogmatic in its approach.'

8. The essential rejoinder that reclaiming the evaluation agenda must be considered at a number of levels within a partnership, including the level of the partnership clientele.

9. The observation that '. . . [partnership] work often generates more questions than answers and highlights needs rather than meeting or resolving them. This may not be what funders want to hear but highlighting of further needs should be seen as an acceptable outcome of evaluation.'

Some of the ideas in this framework will be more relevant than will others, in your particular circumstances at any given time. But, whether adopted in part or as a whole, they seem helpful in persuading you and your partners that:

- The value base, philosophy and methods of working of each partner are adequately incorporated.
- Each partner can reclaim the evaluation agenda.
- All partners thereby demonstrate the impact and value of their work and do not leave it to funders and managers (and other partners).
- All involved also feel that it is worth making the effort to be heard.

But what should I say?

Of course, to decide that our voice has a right to be heard is, however, a different matter from deciding what it is we want to say. For example, if we start out by trying to answer what is perhaps the most obvious question: 'Does this partnership work?' we quickly find that there are a host of subsidiary questions:

- Is the partnership achieving funders' objectives?
- Is the partnership achieving the objectives of each partner?

- Are particular processes set up by the partnership effective?
- Are particular projects set up by the partnership effective?
- Are such projects or processes more effective because of various partners' inputs, or might they be run better by a single agency?
- . . . and so on.

Again we are faced by complexity. To some extent this is reinforced by listening to the range of views we probably all hear about what partnerships in general do well and what they do badly, some of which are summarised here.

Partnership positives

- Bringing different people, agencies and values together
- Focusing them on some shared challenges and opportunities
- Helping us to look at things holistically
- Helping us to look at things from different perspectives
- Helping us to look at things critically
- Helping us to see the need for new projects and processes
- Helping us to build interdisciplinary teams to run them
- Helping us to avoid building overly big structures that cannot quickly respond to change
- Giving us more opportunity to be heard and perhaps to influence others
- Giving us more opportunity to listen
- Delegating some of the politics to more local contexts
- Delegating some of the negotiation and decision-making to those who implement the decisions

Partnership negatives

- Making time management difficult
- Tying us up in endless meetings and secondments
- Distracting agencies away from delivering services
- Making it unclear who is accountable
- Giving too much decision-making power to unelected bureaucrats
- Forcing us to work in unfamiliar contexts
- Forcing us to work in near anarchic contexts
- Driving us to 'grab the dosh and dish out the work.'
- Adding to pressures on already overburdened staff

Clearly there is a wide range of positives and negatives, and some sort of totting up of these and other pluses and minuses may help us develop our thoughts. But the question that we are trying to answer here is not so much whether partnership works in general, but rather *how a particular partnership is helping us*, and how it might be hindering. This involves asking:

- How can we evaluate for our employer whether our partnership is a good thing for them to be engaged in, and what makes it so?
- How can we identify what in a partnership lifts us up and what knocks us down?
- How can we make sense of our partnership work so that it is not only painless but also fulfilling and motivating?
- How can we make our partnership better in ways that matter to us?

Before we set out to do this, let's pause to consider whether our views do indeed matter in the bigger picture.

While services to clients must always be the overriding objective, while value for money is essential if such services are to be sustained, and while political mileage for those brave enough to seek election is unavoidable in a democracy, these goals can only be achieved though workers' efforts. Workers, it is generally agreed, perform better if they value the purpose, context and organisation of their work. Tension, which we have seen is likely to be abundant in any partnership, can be creative. But, if misunderstood or inappropriately channelled, and particularly if accompanied by confusion, it can turn to stress. Stress, as we are all too often reminded in our personal lives, our dealings with colleagues and in newspapers and journals, can undermine the best of plans. So, unless we can make sense of what we are doing in a partnership and attach value to it, our partnership will struggle to thrive. We do indeed need to ask: *'Is partnership working for me?'*

Evaluating the personal benefits of partnership

If we are not careful, Subhra's framework can lead us astray here. Acknowledging different perspectives, increasing involvement, paying attention to intangible aspects, recognising the need for fluidity – all the positive suggestions that he has highlighted to ensure that everyone is heard – might they not get in the way of our thinking clearly about what matters most to ourselves and our employing agency? We may well ask: 'Isn't this task already complicated enough?'

But, unless we acknowledge the sometimes conflicting, sometimes cooperating impulses in ourselves and our partners during our work together, any evaluation will become as inauthentic as a partnership itself that pretends they don't exist. No matter how hard we try to make sense of the inauthentic, it will not fit into our ideas. We wear ourselves down – and out – as our thinking continuously yields no sense.

Returning to Subhra's suggestions with this in mind, we find that perhaps they can actually help! If we recognise each of our partners' views as the components of a complex entity, reflect on how they interlink, and then evaluate each of them, we can build up a useful picture. On the other hand, judgements made about any partnership as a whole will probably be open to question when set in the discrete contexts of its component parts. Moreover, overarching views will be all too likely to invite challenge and criticism: partners who are unhappy at being excluded from an evaluation are likely to become hostile if they are the object of judgements that don't make sense to them.

Within partnerships (as within families), work and benefits are always distributed unevenly. It is important to allow members to express their views about such unequal distribution even though they may have no wish to change it.

Practice Focus 6.2

Dan looked very tired and fed up at the start of the partnership awayday. During a team-building exercise, the facilitator discovered that Dan was the 'engine' that made the partnership vehicle move. Everybody was asked to comment on this, including Dan. He stated that he did feel 'taken for granted' from time to time, but he was willing to occupy this role within the partnership. Dan expressed renewed enthusiasm and commitment at the end of the day, even though nothing had changed in objective terms.

In short, legitimising the right for each partner to be heard stresses the importance for each partner to speak in their own distinct voice, rather than try to speak about the partnership as a whole. Again, we come back to the question of *how each partner can make up their own minds* about what our being in a partnership is good for, and how it might help us more fully.

Speaking with my voice

The overriding message here is that, in partnership, you must be prepared to make contributions in ways that your partners can comprehend and absorb. The confidence that you need in order to do this will be enhanced if you develop a strong voice for yourself, in conjunction with the colleagues and clients you are representing in your partnership work. So, we are deliberately going to present, without further guidance, what may be challenging questions for you to answer. You may be in partnership, and we may be trying to help you, but some things you have to decide for yourself.

Some sort of framework for thought becomes ever more important. We offer this one. Throughout words such as 'I', 'my' and 'mine' are shorthand for talking about your employing agency.

Is partnership helping me?

My objectives
What are my overall objectives? (those that shape all my work, in a partnership and elsewhere.)

My objectives in partnership
On which of these objectives does my partnership work have any impact?

How?

The benefits of partnership
Which partners help me achieve my objectives?

Would they have this impact if we were not working in partnership?

What benefits have accrued from new objectives being added during my partnership work?

The hindrances of partnership
Which partners hinder the achievement of my objectives?

Is this made worse because we are working in partnership?

Has there been any cost to my taking on new objectives?

What cost?

My influence on my partners

Have I influenced my partners' objectives in ways that make them closer to my own?

Have I been able to give them information that they would not otherwise have obtained?

Have I been able to present them with arguments that they would not otherwise have heard?

The value of partnership

Am I getting what I want out of the relationship?

Where am I 'winning' in the partnership game?

Where am I 'losing'?

The effectiveness of partnership

Is any such gain worth the effort?

What extra resources have had to be expended to achieve it?

Could it have been achieved for less effort in some other way?

How?

The development of partnership

How can I build on what partnership has helped me achieve?

What can I do about those aspects of partnership where I am 'losing'?

Of course, only a few (if any) of these questions are going to have entirely straightforward answers. So, each of them needs to be approached with a view to not only collating opinions and data, but also recognising that you will have to make value judgements if you are to convey a meaningful message when you speak up.

Hearing others

In all parts of our partnership work we can rest assured (and constantly need to remember) that, whatever we are thinking about our partners' actions and motives, they will be thinking much the same about us in turn. So, having established our right to be heard and having outlined how to speak up clearly, we need to hold all of that clearly in one compartment of our minds, while in another we respect the rights of our partners to do the same. Again, this can become complicated, and something approaching partnership paranoia can set in, if we are not careful:

- Sometimes our partners will act in a spirit of mutual aid and sometimes out of self-interest.
- We need to be on our guard against partners who may, from time to time, act without regard for, or indeed in opposition to, our interests.

- We nevertheless need to keep up our guard in ways that do not promote hostility where none existed, or exacerbate what might have been a minor suspicion.
- Partners may rebuff our genuine offers of help, unless we balance them with respect for their rights and abilities to look after their own interests.

Should we try to work out how each of our partners sees us when they develop their own voice as we have just done to develop and present our views about them? There can be some benefit in trying to see ourselves as others see us. It can show concern and respect. It can perhaps help us avoid making mistakes. It might help us uncover hidden agendas and avoid being manipulated. But, it also carries the risk of being presumptuous, of preferring to reach our own conclusions rather than listening to those developed by others, of being seen thereby to be disrespectful at the very moment that we are trying to do otherwise.

Perhaps the best course is to:

- Assess quietly to ourselves how we think others see us.
- Keep our conclusions to ourselves.
- Actively elicit their views on such matters.
- Think constructively about what it means when our expectations are not matched by our partners' stated opinions.

In conclusion, if we come to a partnership expecting to gain from it, or even just being told that we ought to expect to gain from it, we need to assess whether we are helping or hindering our partners with an effort equal to that we are prepared to put into assessing whether they are helping or hindering us.

If the partnership is to work, we must recognise the importance of, and express clearly, our self-interest and its underpinning values, but we must also acknowledge that they will be difficult to reinforce outside a context and spirit of mutual aid. This leads us to ask:

- How an evaluation built on an understanding of mutual rights and responsibilities can help make a partnership better.
- What is to be done to further this.

Practice Focus 6.3

Kathleen raised the question of evaluation under the heading of 'any other business' at the end of a long and tiring partnership meeting. The result was not a very positive one. Some people made their excuses and left, while others remained quiet while Kathleen struggled to try and generate some interest and enthusiasm. She realised that she had made a mistake in introducing such a big, complex topic at the end of a long meeting. She therefore suggested that they should put the topic on the agenda for the next meeting so that they could give it the attention it deserved. Gary, who had attended the same conference as Kathleen, suggested that they should prepare a discussion paper based on the conference and present this at the next meeting. Kathleen welcomed this supportive gesture but realised it was going to be difficult to produce a paper that did justice to the complexities.

Improving services by evaluating in partnership

Whenever we evaluate a partnership it is always important to ask why we are doing it at that specific time:

- Is it because someone requires it – for example, our boss or a funding agency?
- Is it to answer a criticism, perhaps from a partner or client?
- Is it to decide whether to tie a knot or, alternatively, to move on?
- Is it to try to make keeping going less painful?

All these are valid reasons and often more than one will apply. But, whatever our personal concerns and, whatever the demands of our funders and controllers, it is always important to remember that partnership is pointless unless it can be justified by the service it provides to our clients.

There will almost always be those who can challenge what we are doing, who can suggest what they regard as a better way, and who will draw attention to our shortcomings. This is as true in partnership working as in almost everything else. But, if we can find a way ourselves to strive constantly to do better, to improve what we are offering to our clients – or at least to offer it more efficiently – we will always find it easier to answer criticisms, accommodate constructive change and maintain our sense of well-being.

Managing partnership evaluation

From several of the discussions earlier in this book (for example, on leadership in Chapter 1), it can be argued that managing a partnership is difficult, if not impossible. We have to focus on managing ourselves, our agencies and our relationships with each of our partners. If we try to do more, we turn partnership into something else, more akin to a merger or takeover. Or, we have to set up a specific project within the partnership in which we have agreed to delegate powers and subordinate values for a specific limited purpose and for a set period of time. Given this constraint on managing a partnership, how can we improve services by evaluating in partnership?

Experiential learning consultant, Roger Greenaway (2001), has suggested that, rather than trying to evaluate everything all at once, it is better to:

- Evaluate little and often.
- Evaluate different things at different times on a planned, rolling agenda.
- Focus on different people's perspectives at different stages of the evaluation.
- Give different people the chance to present their views at the various stages.

He has written (Greenaway, 1993) to illustrate these ideas: 'the constant reviewing . . . was in reality the most important aspect' (p115) and 'in the end we were learning more from each other than from the teacher' (p114). Greenaway works mostly with young people, but adopting his approach has the potential to turn the inherent difficulties of managing a whole-partnership evaluation into the virtues of building into an evaluation the rights of various partners to be heard, in a way that is consistent with Subhra's framework.

Of course, such an approach is different from, and possibly in addition to, evaluations requested by funders and managers who want 'answers' and a clear and comprehensive accounting. But, undertaking a little-and-often rolling programme can be organised in such a way as to make completion of such a global evaluation easier. A sudden demand for a big report can result in partners becoming emotionally fraught. In contrast, things can be less likely to be overlooked or voices go unheard if partners become accustomed to hearing each other regularly, evaluate their own and others' contributions – and evidence can be stored as you go, rather than gathered in a last-minute rush.

Negotiating the agenda: making judgements or making changes

Will funders and managers be happy with an evaluation pieced together over time from multiple perspectives, containing possibly contradictory views? Perhaps not. But, if Subhra's advice is kept in mind, and negotiation with funders and managers is undertaken in good faith, you can remind those who have advocated partnership (or even made it a condition of funding) that, if there had not been multiple views at the outset, then a partnership would not have been necessary – and that silencing differing views is not really something that you can advocate. But beyond this, if you can project and then demonstrate that a little-and-often rolling programme of evaluation will deliver data and improvements, you will have strong grounds for expecting a supportive response when you negotiate with your funders, managers and partners.

The separate issue of subjectivity may also be raised. Isn't an evaluation with such heavy emphasis on giving each partner their voice going to run the risk of being self-congratulatory? Might it sit uncomfortably with those who must strive to account without bias to politicians and the electorate on money that they spend? Might you even anticipate a challenge from those, such as academics and accountants, for whom evaluation is traditionally their turf? We suggest that you encourage them to proceed in a spirit of partnership. Some will hopefully have already adopted many of the ideas and principles set out here. Those who can undertake evaluation work in a way that encourages participation and empowerment may well find themselves much sought after.

But beyond even this, when we look at evaluation as a tool for making improvements, the potential difficulties over subjectivity can be turned into a virtue. Heisenberg's uncertainty principle in molecular physics (Heisenberg, 1958) and the Hawthorne effect in social science both lead to the conclusion that you cannot measure something without changing it in some way. Subhra makes this same point when he says that 'values inevitably impinge on the evaluative process' (p72). The implication of this is that pure objectivity is impossible. If a core purpose of evaluation is to make change and improvement, this would seem to shift productive debate from asking whether evaluation can be objective to asking how it can make change.

Above all, doing it this way offers opportunities to motivate and empower partners to make improvement and change. How else can we increase motivation and a sense of empowerment?

Blaming or acclaiming?

In an undertaking where there are quite clearly 'others', it can be very tempting to hold them responsible for what goes wrong. A blame culture can develop. Ways to win arguments and gain power can be sought through destructive rather than constructive criticisms.

Good things can come out of picking over the pieces of a wreckage, deconstructing disasters so as to make sure they don't happen again. The history of the development of the welfare state can be written in precisely this way: horror – reaction – change, as can the development of the Human Rights Act 1998 (Crompton and Thompson, 2000). Similarly, when a train crashes, we react by asking whether it was because our expectations for avoiding a crash were not met, or because those expectations for the train operator's performance were not adequately established. We seek to apportion blame. We feel dissatisfied if no-one can be held responsible.

Sometimes this need to apportion blame can be experienced negatively within the partnership, leading to tension, low morale and a block to creative working. But avenues to improvement can also be pursued proactively, rather than just reactively. Rather than waiting for a train to crash, we can constantly reassure ourselves that the great majority of them do not. We can reinforce the things we are doing well and try to predict where doing more might avert things going wrong. The pieces of a jigsaw begin to fall into place that suggests approaching evaluation of partnership in a way that:

- Is done continuously, or at least regularly and often.
- Looks at different times at different parts of the partnership, its projects and processes.
- Takes account of the perspectives of different partners and funders and evaluators.
- Is clearly designed to make improvements.
- Is not set up just to pick over and eliminate negatives but, above all, to reinforce positives and develop new ones.

The parts of partnership

If, then, we want to evaluate different parts of a partnership at different times, how can we best divide a partnership into sections that will lend themselves usefully to such a programme of evaluation?

The most obvious parts of a partnership that need to be monitored are those tied in to funding, whether that funding is provided by an external agency or by one of the partners themselves. Quite often portions of such funding are released on completion of interim evaluations, and successful reports to one funder can open doors to funding from others. There may be those of us who feel that our work is so important and our cause so just that we should receive financial backing from government as a right, without having constantly to remake our case. However, there are very few (if any) areas of activity where this is still the case, even in areas of high public profile such as health, education and policing.

But, despite the sometimes seemingly heavy weight of these obligations, partners should not undertake the task of fulfilling their work passively. On the one hand, Subhra has suggested that funders may be willing to negotiate their criteria for assessment. On the other, partners can work out amongst themselves how they are going to work together to gather and present the material that the funder has requested. Simply put, this task does not have to be undertaken by one big agency on such a rushed deadline that their partners have no opportunity to comment or contribute.

Indeed, if the evaluation and reporting requirement are approached in a more positive spirit, ways may be found to work together to achieve multiple goals all at the same time, thereby decreasing overall workloads, and perhaps improving partnership operations. If this is to be the case, or at least have a chance of being so, the key almost certainly lies in following Greenaway's advice, as set out above – the implementation of a 'little-and-often' programme whereby each partner starts early in the partnership to present and evaluate things that they can monitor and report without unusual effort. In such circumstances, there would seem to be reasonable hope of various partners identifying how these building blocks can be gradually pieced together (perhaps by increasingly complex cooperative effort) into giving the funders what they want.

> *We looked at rock climbing in different ways. First there was how I did it and how I felt – not too good, as it happens. Everyone went through that. Then we all discussed how we thought each other had done – which surprised me, as quite a few thought I had done okay. Finally we got round to thinking how we had all helped each other as a group, and how it was easier to take help from some people than from others.*

Greenaway, 1993; p114.

The alternative, of course, would be a heavily planned model, whereby someone takes on the responsibility of deciding how the funders' requests are broken down into pieces and who is allocated what to do. No matter how well such an approach is managed, it will run a considerable risk of generating argument more than cooperation, and perhaps instil the habits of a 'command' organisation rather than a partnership approach.

Practice Focus 6.4

As a senior manager from the lead agency in the project, Steve had been asked to chair the partnership. When he received a letter from the principal funding body requesting a report, at relatively short notice, evaluating the project's progress to date, he took it upon himself to write the report on behalf of the partnership. The first that other partners knew about this was when, at the next partnership meeting, Steve circulated a copy of his report. This produced a very strong negative reaction that totally took Steve by surprise. He genuinely thought that partners would be pleased that he had been so efficient in completing the report and saving others the trouble of having to deal with it. Steve learned the hard way that evaluation of a partnership needs to be done in the spirit of partnership, taking on board everyone's views, not just those of the more powerful members.

In view of this we would suggest starting out your evaluation in partnership as early as possible by giving each partner an opportunity to present an evaluation of their own work. This can be followed in the next round by letting them make a presentation on what they have achieved against their own objectives since the partnership work began. Then, combinations of agencies can work together to evaluate and present how they have supported (and possibly hindered) each other in their combined approach to their objectives.

Later, once a partnership has set up formal projects (operated by teams with specific powers and budgets delegated by groups of partners, and working towards negotiated objectives) multi-partner teams could report on what they have accomplished in the context of such a project. In a similar vein, if formally structured processes have been set up to be run by two or more partners, with a clear expectation that other partners participate in regular and consistent ways, evaluations of these could be presented on a reasonably regular basis.

Throughout all this ongoing work together to negotiate, on a continuous basis, which components of your partnership's achievements are to be part of its rolling programme of evaluation, it is worth referring back to key points in Subhra's framework relating to clarification of possibly multiple purposes; recognition of intangibles; openness to new objectives; inclusion of views from several levels – especially clients.

If only to guard against the idea that we may be giving undue weight to such matters, it is important to stress that each component of evaluation would also need to look at the issues that evaluations are expected to ask. Such as:

- Were objectives achieved?
- Were they achieved efficiently?
- Were they achieved within budget?
- Were they achieved within the intended timeframe?
- Were other legal obligations adequately addressed?
- Were all such achievements sustainable?

We would contend that such questions are best set in multiple, often complex and sometimes changing contexts, if lasting benefits are to be obtained.

Deconstructing partnership workings

Alongside an evaluation of what is achieved, it will almost certainly be useful to anyone who wants to improve their partnership, to ask how you achieved it. As a starting point, you can try to work this out in the context of each significant achievement that is presented in your evaluations. Such an approach would probably have the virtue of letting partners' understandings of their complex interorganisational workings develop organically. Subhra here proposes integrating evaluation in such a way as to be able to assess how closely:

> *Evaluation priorities and activities integrate into the various functions of . . . [a partnership's] routine operations . . . [These might include] planning, policy making, recruitment and selection, supervision and appraisal systems, equal opportunities policies and systems, staff development and training, public relations, fund-raising strategies and so on.*
>
> p75.

Each, Subhra argues, 'offer opportunities for evaluation to feature significantly and an audit may uncover some useful ways in which the profile of evaluation could be raised' (ibid.).

Each is certainly worth attention in a rolling programme of evaluation. But rather than analyse each of these in turn, we leave you instead a list of alternative suggestions on how the idea might be adapted and developed.

Does our list, set out below, more usefully begin to describe the way partners work together than a comparable breakdown of a more traditional organisation's departments (for example, planning and policy, service delivery, personnel, public relations, support services)? If so, what might usefully be added?

- information-gathering and information-sharing
- consultation
- empowerment
- participation
- negotiation
- interpartner skills development
- partner development

- multipartner project management
- multipartner process management
- interorganisational finance management
- fund-raising and fund-sharing

It is worth taking time to think on this carefully. What from this list seems to cause difficulty in the way you work together? Would an evaluation help? What in the way you work together seems to go well? Are there lessons that can be reinforced and applied elsewhere? Following a more traditional breakdown might be a safer way of ensuring that everything is covered and thus reaping the benefits of integration that Subhra has talked about. Developing new ways of looking at a partnership's inner working, as we have begun to develop here, might bring fresh thinking to bear on old and new challenges. And we hope they will bring success.

Celebrating partnership

As partners we decided to write this book very largely in response to the pressures and strains that we were all experiencing in our partnership work, and which were mirrored elsewhere. For a while our personal pressures got worse. There were times when we wondered how we could accommodate the differing views we held. There were times when we had to accept that cherished views were not as clear as we originally thought. At the end, what we have achieved is not perfect. It has raised more questions than it has answered, but we got the job done. Along the way, as we asked for comment on various sections, the feedback often mirrored our own views, developed as we worked together. Trying to work out in partnership what working in partnership is all about had helped each of us not only to increase our knowledge and understanding of partnership, but also to identify and begin to learn new skills.

Each of us has learned a great deal about how to cope with several of partnership's pitfalls and we have come to recognise more clearly partnership's many potentials. We very much hope that those of you who are now reading what we have done, and have kept going in partnership with us this far, will benefit in similar ways. Can we now go further and actually celebrate, not only what we have done, but also what others who are working in partnerships can do?

After all, we celebrate democracy, but who can say that it works perfectly? Rather like partnership, democracy can sometimes seem like rather hard work, with lots of people sounding off at each other and endless meetings where the wrangling seems to be more about gaining the upper hand than delivering what people want. But we celebrate it. So can't we stand up to jibes such as that from the Audit Commission when they ask: 'How many partnership's does it take to . . . ?' (1999, p54). But, before the celebrations of your partnership begin, we offer a few tips for safer partying.

Celebration and affirmation

We explored earlier how overarching views will be all too likely to invite challenge and criticism; that partners who are unhappy at being excluded from an evaluation are likely to become hostile if they are the object of judgements that do not make sense to them. This can be as true of praise as it is of criticism. So, it can offer important advice when our celebration is to be backed by a public statement, such as a press release.

Media guidebooks often offer very helpful advice, but not all of it may be useful for partnerships. For example, the one issued by Dorset County Council (2001) at the time this chapter was being written recommends, alongside guidance on the benefits of focusing on one or two key messages and delivering those messages in reasonably simple language:

- A consistent corporate image.
- The need for careful monitoring to ensure consistency in the message.

At the very least it needs to be asked amongst partners whether each of them wants to be party to a consistent embracing image, and whether they want to give up the hard-won right to speak with their own voice to ensure consistency of message. While it is advisable to keep the media informed in order to stop other messages about us from filling a news vacuum, partners need to be careful not to give inappropriate impressions that they speak for their partners. Sometimes partners may agree to delegate authority over their public relations – for example, on clearly constituted projects within a partnership. Otherwise, partners should be left to speak for themselves, perhaps in due time volunteering to participate in a process whereby they will not make (negative) statements about each other without consulting first.

Just as care needs to be taken about not doing our partners' celebrating for them, we need to be equally careful about neglecting to mention them. This can be awkward. Much as our announcements may contain lengthy attributions and lots of logos, the media are not going to mention the whole lot. Strong statements about 'essential roles played by our partners' have a far higher chance of being reported, even more so if those roles can be described in a factual and newsworthy way. If this involves naming some but not all partners, each of us will do well to keep some sort of account of how often we mention each other so as to ensure that we are even-handed. Explaining any such practice to all our partners is probably going to help.

Practice Focus 6.5

Steve had learned his lesson (about the dangers of acting unilaterally in a partnership) from the criticism he received for undertaking an evaluation without consultation. So, when the time to issue a press release came, he was very careful to draft it *with* the partnership rather than *for* it. However, it was very unfortunate that, while the press release listed all the partners involved, that actual item that appeared in the local newspaper only mentioned two of them. At the next partnership meeting it was accepted that this was not Steve's fault and they looked carefully at how they might try to avoid this problem with future press releases or indeed publicity of any kind.

Diplomatic protocols

Similar considerations will probably reap benefits of improved partnership working when you are working on things like: guest lists; orders of speaking at public engagements; nomenclature; and so on.

Our language and our gestures can, however, go beyond such essential, if somewhat formal niceties. An overemphasis on 'getting it right' can make praise sound empty. Two things can usefully be done. The first is to use language and behaviour that recognise and acknowledge what helps foster a spirit of partnership. The second is to be authentic and, if possible, heartfelt.

Language that reinforces the sort of behaviour we probably all seek in our partners might include some of the following. We offer it not as a comprehensive source, but as something that we hope will spark your own ideas:

- communication
- emotional intelligence and honesty
- civility
- shared acceptance of mission
- comfort in agreeing to disagree
- clarity of lines of demarcation
- referrals
- breadth and quality of new ideas
- transparency of decisions
- opportunity for redress
- equality of opportunity
- sustainability and support
- humour

In a similar vein, just as we do not want to provide a 'partner's lexicon' for you, nor do we want to tell you how to be heartfelt. We could tell you to look people in the eye, but not to be too obvious about it. We could tell you to greet partners with a handshake, but not become flesh-pressers. But do we need to tell you? Can't most of us tell whether politicians or football managers in post-match interviews, or 'real life TV' game show contestants mean what they say? So, let's not be phoney! Above all let's not try to represent partnership as something it is not.

If partnership is a bit chaotic and sometimes a bit frustrating, let's not say otherwise. If sometimes it can be a bit painful, and you have to work your way through it, let's not pretend that it doesn't sometimes hurt. Sometimes we just have to let a partnership follow its course, ride with it, and say: 'That's partnership!'

Let's not claim to be in charge of a partnership when we can't be. No-one can. But let's not be afraid of saying that we are undertaking important work in our partnership, that we're striving to make improvements in the ways that we work with our partners, and that this can probably be to the significant benefit of those we seek to serve.

Avoid overindulgence

No matter how good you become at this art, and regardless of whether your words and actions are heartfelt in your praise of partnership, beware of overdoing it! Whether you are talking to – or writing for, or partying with – elected representatives, or your boss, or an external evaluator, it is important always to think about how those you are trying to help would see you.

No matter how hard we have had to struggle to make partnership work, no matter what we have had to learn to make partnership painless, no matter that we know the partnership won't work unless the partners are valued and nurtured, for those outside the partnership, partnership is the medium not the message. And here, in contradiction to McLuhan's famous maxim that the medium is the message, the medium is *not* the message that people will want to hear. Partnership is the approach through which what people want can be delivered, rather than what people want. So, as we celebrate partnership – or rather, as we celebrate our partners – above all we celebrate their achievement and the people such achievement has helped.

Conclusion

And – when the celebrations are over – remember what we learned in this chapter:

- That it is important for each of us to take the time to take stock of what we value in the partnerships in which we are involved.
- That each partner has not only a right to be heard in any evaluation of a partnership, but also a duty to speak up about what matters to them.
- That partners need to listen as well as speak.
- That evaluating part of a partnership is more likely to be of value than evaluating a partnership as a whole, or trying to decide whether 'partnership is a good thing'.
- That the over-riding reason for evaluation should be to strive to do better.
- That achieving the goal of doing better is more likely to be achieved if partners take stock regularly and often, in participative ways, than if an outsider tries to address everything at once . . . but it should be added that outside help can often be beneficial.
- That partnership is sometimes chaotic and frustrating – like democracy – and can sometimes even be painful, but partners can work their way through.
- That success in the hard work of partnership is something worth celebrating, but not at the expense of losing sight of those whom a partnership is striving to help.

Conclusion

Baxter and Toon (2001) recognise that current systems of service delivery are increasingly partnership-based in so far as they require close collaboration between different professionals and disciplines. They quote the work of Davis (2000) when they argue that:

> All participants bring equally valid knowledge and expertise from their professional and personal experience and that a 'diverse group can arrive at a place no individual and no like-minded group would have achieved'.
>
> p271.

This, in effect, is the basis of partnership as the model for so much public service delivery in the early parts of the twenty-first century: the idea that people can achieve more by working together than they can by struggling on alone.

Certainly this is a premise that we would agree with. However, what we feel the need to add by way of qualification is that, while we can achieve more together than apart, the actual operations of partnerships are very complex indeed, and not without their problems. We would certainly not want to reinforce the simplistic view that partnership is merely a matter of getting people around the same table, as if this will somehow magically eliminate tensions and conflicts and establish a consensus. Nor would we want to support the misleading view of partnership as unquestionably a good thing. We are well aware that badly run or ill-conceived partnerships can do considerable harm to the people within the partnership, the organisations they represent, and, of course, the people they are seeking to serve.

What we want to promote is a view of partnership as basically a good thing, but something that needs to be carefully thought through, very sensitively and skilfully handled and undertaken in a genuine spirit of collaboration and commitment to shared goals.

Working in partnership can be hard going. It can also be very frustrating or even painful work. Of course, there is a certain irony in naming this book, *Partnership Made Painless*, as we are well aware that there can be no guarantees of pain-free partnership working. When you bring people together, there will always be the potential for someone (or everyone) to get hurt. Our aim, of course, has not been to offer meaningless guarantees or empty reassurances, but rather to identify the main sources of difficulty (and thus potential pain) and to offer guidance on how you may wish to proceed in such ways that seek to avoid or minimise such pain.

That guidance has taken two forms. Where we have felt able to offer practical advice based on our own experiences and our understanding of the complex dynamics of partnership working, we have done so. In other places we have recognised that it would be dangerous to offer practical advice without understanding the particular nuances of your particular situation, and so we have posed a number of questions for you to consider. We present these questions as a means of helping to stimulate thought, debate and analysis in order to help you feel better equipped to deal with the complexities. So, while some people may feel disappointed that we have asked more questions than we have answered, we see it as a positive that we have done so.

We cannot take those complexities away, for such is partnership, nor can we give you simple guidelines to follow that will ensure you are able to deal with these complexities. However, what we can do – and what we hope we have done – is to help guide your thinking about these matters, stimulate further reflection and encourage a positive but realistic approach to the challenges involved.

We have not presented a 'theory' of partnership in any formal sense, although our approach is clearly based on a number of concepts and principles. We recognise that the book is far from comprehensive in its coverage of either theory or practice, but our aim has never been to provide the last word on the subject. Indeed, we recognise that we have only touched upon points that could form the basis of a book in their own right – power, for example. We hope that our efforts will encourage readers to read widely on the subject, to take it seriously as an issue that requires a lot of thought (for example, by recognising training needs in this area) and to face the challenges in a more informed way.

We have tried to be fair in presenting both the benefits of partnership and the perils and pitfalls. Working in partnership can be very challenging, but it can also be very rewarding. We wish you well in rising to the challenges and reaping the rewards.

Guide to Further Study

Tennyson (1998) is a very useful guide to partnership working, offering both practical advice and food for thought to stimulate further debate, analysis and learning. Sullivan and Skelcher (2001) is a book which does a good job of setting partnership in its broader policy context.

Although, as we have indicated, there are significant differences between teamwork and partnership, the team development literature can none the less offer some useful insights into some aspects of partnership working. Payne (2000) and Dearling (2000) are worth consulting.

There are various books on working in partnership in specific contexts. Here is a selection: Murphy (2004) provides a useful account of partnership working in child protection. Roaf (2002) explores the history of joined-up working post Children Act (1989) and offers suggestions for its development. Murphy has also edited a book with Fiona Harbin (2000) looking at partnership between child protection and substance abuse teams. Burnett and Appleton (2003) describe and analyse working together in the youth justice system. Walker (2003) offers a training manual for anyone working in adolescent mental health. Connexions (2001) have a useful guide to 'who does what' in work with young people. Wheal (2000) stresses the value of learning from other people's experience when working together with parents. Elvin and Marlow (1998) describe a successful crime reduction partnership. Horwath and Shardlow (2003) offer insight and guidance to making links between different social work specialisms.

Effective partnership working depends on good people skills. These are well covered in Thompson (2002). Among such people skills, a primary role is taken by communication skills and these are addressed in some detail in Thompson (2003b).

The importance of 'partnership brokering' and leadership is helpfully presented in Tennyson and Wilde (2000).

Chapter 6 draws heavily on the work of Subhra (2001). We reproduce here the full set of references and recommended reading from that paper.

1. These are used by Subhra to chart the historic and conceptual development of evaluation:

Armstrong, J. and Key, M. (1979) Evaluation, Change and Community Work. *Community Development Journal.* 14: 3.

Dale, R. (1998) *Evaluation Frameworks for Development Programmes and Projects.* Sage.

Dixon, J. and Sindall, C. (1994) Applying Logics of Change to the Evaluation of Community Development in Health Promotion. *Health Promotion International.* 9: 4.

Edmonds, J. (Ed.) (1999) *Health Promotion with Young People: An Introductory Guide to Evaluation.* Health Education Authority.

Esttrella, M. and Gaventa, J. (1998) *Who Counts Reality? Participatory Monitoring and Evaluation: A Literature Review.* IDS working paper no. 70, IDS.

Everitt, A. and Hardiker, P. (1996) *Evaluating for Good Practice.* Macmillan.

House, E. R. (Ed.) (1986) *New Directions in Educational Evaluation.* Falmer.

Maslow, A. (1973) *The Farther Reaches of Human Nature.* Penguin.

Meyrick, J. and Sinkler, P. (1999) *An Evaluation Resource for Healthy Living Centres.* Health Education Authority.

Rubin, F. (1995) *A Basic Guide to Evaluation for Development Workers.* Oxfam.

Russell, J. (1998) *The Purpose of Evaluation; Different Ways of Seeing Evaluation; Self-Evaluation; Involving Users in Evaluation; Performance Indicators: Use and Misuse; Using Evaluation to Explore Policy.* Discussion papers, Charities Evaluation Service.

Subhra, G. and Chauhan, V. (1999) *Developing Black Services.* Alcohol Concern.

Taylor, M. (1995) *Unleashing the Potential: Bringing Residents to the Centre of Regeneration.* Joseph Rowntree Foundation.

Van Der Eyken, W. (1993) *Managing Evaluation.* Charities Evaluation Service.

Weiss, C.H. (Ed.) (1986) The Stakeholder Approach to Evaluation: Origins and Promise, in House, E. (Ed.) *New Directions in Educational Evaluation.* Falmer.

2. These are recommended by Subhra for developing further his recommendations for action:

Dixon, J. (1995) Community Stories and Indicators for Evaluating Community Development. *Community Development Journal.* 30: 4.

Feuerstein, M. T. (1986) *Partners in Evaluation: Evaluating Development and Community Programmes with Participants.* Macmillan.

References

Audit Commission (1999) *A Life's Work: Local Authorities, Economic Development and Economic Regeneration.* Audit Commission Publications.

Barnes, P. (2002) *Leadership with Young People.* Russell House Publishing.

Baxter, C. (Ed.) (2001) *Managing Diversity and Inequality in Health Care.* Baillière Tindall.

Baxter, C. and Toon, P. (2001) Nurses, Doctors and the Meaning of Holism: Interprofessionalism and Values in Primary Care, in Baxter, C. (2001).

Berne, E (1963) *The Structure and Dynamics of Organisations and Groups.* Lippincott.

Blair, T. (1997) Speech at the launch of the Social Exclusion Unit. Cabinet Office.

Blair, T. (1998) *Leading the Way: A New Vision for Local Government.* IPPR.

Brechin, A., Brown, H. and Eby, M. (Eds.) (2000) *Critical Practice in Health and Social Care.* Sage.

Burnett, R. and Appleton, C. (2002) Crossing Occupational Borders in a Youth Offending Team. Paper presented at the British Society of Criminology conference, July.

Burnett, R. and Appleton, C. (2003) *Joined-up Youth Justice.* Russell House Publishing.

Cabinet Office (1999) *Modernising Government.* Cm 4310. The Stationery Office.

Chapman, T. (2000) *Time to Grow: A Comprehensive Programme for People Working With Young Offenders and Young People at Risk.* Russell House Publishing.

Charles, M. and Hendry, E. (Eds.) (2000) *Training Together to Safeguard Children.* NSPCC/PIAT.

Connexions (2001) *A Reference Guide: Social Policy and Agency Practice: Who Does What?* Connexions.

Crawford, A. (1997) *The Local Governance of Crime: Appeals to Community and Partnerships.* Oxford University Press.

Crompton, I. and Thompson, N. (2000) *The Human Rights Act 1998: A Training Resource Pack.* Learning Curve Publishing.

Davis, C. (2000) Vive la Difference: That's What Will Make Collaboration Work. *Nursing Times.* 96: 15.

Dean, H. and Woods, R. (Eds.) (1999) *Social Policy Review 11.* Social Policy Association.

Dearling, A. (2000) *Effective Use of Teambuilding in Social Welfare Organisations.* Russell House Publishing.

DETR (2000) *Joining It Up Locally.* Report of PAT Team 17, The Stationery Office.

Dobson, A. (2002) Who Wears the Crown? *Community Care.* 13 June.

DoH (1997) *The New NHS.* The Stationery Office.

DoH (1998a) *Our Healthier Nation.* The Stationery Office.

DoH (1998b) *Partnership in Action.* Department of Health.

DoH (1998d) *Modernising Social Services.* The Stationery Office.

DoH (1999a) *Saving Lives.* The Stationery Office.

DoH (1999b)*Working Together to Safeguard Children:A Guide to Interagency Working to Safeguard and Promote the Welfare of Children.* The Stationery Office.

DoH (2000) *The NHS Plan.* The Stationery Office.

Dorset County Council. *Making the most of our news.* Dorset County Council.

Ellis, J. (2000) Chairing the ACPC. *Bolton ACPC Newsletter.*

Elvin, A. and Marlow, A. (1998) Stranger to Servant: A Durable Model of Community Safety Partnership, in Marlow, A. and Pitts, J. (1998).

Employment Service (1999) *Getting Partnerships Right*. Seminar held at Ranmoor Hall.

Factor, F. et al. (2001) *The RHP Companion to Working with Young People*. Russell House Publishing.

Gallagher, C. (2002) Book review of 'Leadership with Young People'. *Newscheck*. June.

Gilbert, P. and Thompson, N. (2002) *Supervision and Leadership Skills: A Training Resource Pack*. Learning Curve Publishing.

Goldson, B. (2000) *The New Youth Justice*. Russell House Publishing.

Gordon, L. (1989) *Heroes of their Own Lives*. Virago.

Graham, J. (1997) *Outdoor Leadership*. The Mountaineers.

Greenaway, R. (1993) *Playback: A Guide to Reviewing Activities*. The Duke of Edinburgh's Award.

Greenaway, R. (2001) Personal correspondence.

Greig, R. (2000) What Happened to Teamwork? *Community Care*. 23 March.

Harbin, F. and Murphy, M. (2000) *Substance Misuse and Child Care*. Russell House Publishing.

Heisenberg, W. (1958) *The Physicist's Conception of Human Nature*. Hutchinson.

Hewson, J. and Turner, C. (1992) *Transactional Analysis in Management*. The Staff College.

Horwath, J. and Shardlow, S. (2003) *Making Links Across Specialisms*. Russell House Publishing.

Howard, R. (1994) *Across the Divide*. DoH.

Home Office (1950) *Children Neglected or Ill-treated in their Own Homes*. Joint circular Ministry of Health and Ministry of Education, HMSO.

Hudson, B. (1999) Dismantling the Berlin Wall: Developments at the Health-Social Care Interface, in Dean, H. and Woods, R. (1999).

Hudson, B. (2000) Inter-agency Collaboration: A Sceptical View. in Brechin, A. et al. (2000).

Hunter, M. (2000) Is Compact a Help to Joint Working? *Community Care*. 21 December.

Hunter, M. (2001) Will Social Services Suffer in New Regime? *Community Care*. 23 August.

Hutchinson, J. and Campbell, M. (1998) Working in Partnerships: Lessons from the Literature. Research Report 63. DfEE.

Hutton, J. (2001) News item. *Community Care*. 15 February.

Hyden, M. (2001) For the Child's Sake. *Child and Family Social Work*. 6: 2, pp115-28.

Ingram, G. and Harris, J. (2001) *Delivering Good Youth Work*. Russell House Publishing.

Kotter, J. P. and Schlesinger, L. A. (1986) Choosing Strategies for Change, in Mayon-White, B.(1986).

Laming, P. (2003) *The Victoria Climbie Inquiry*. (Cm 5730). HMSO.

Liddle, A. M. and Bottoms, A. E. (1994) *The Five Towns Initiative: Key Findings and Implications from a Retrospective Research Analysis*. Home Office.

Liddle, A. and Gelsttrope, L. (1994) Crime Prevention and Inter-agency Co-operation. Crime Prevention Unit Paper 53, Police Research Group.

Marlow, A. and Pitts, J. (1998) *Planning Safer Communities*. Russell House Publishing.

Maslow, W. (1973) *The Farther Reaches of Human Nature*. Penguin.

Mayon-White, B. (Ed.) (1986) *Planning and Managing Change*. Harper and Row.

McKeown, K. (2001) *Partnerships: Principles, Pragmatism and Practice: Why? What? How?* Conference notes, NW Lancs. Health Authority.

Mintzberg, H. et al. (1996) Some Surprising Things About Collaboration: Knowing How People Connect Makes it Work Better. *Organisational Dynamics*, spring pp60–70.

Moore, J. (1992) *The ABC of Child Protection*. Arena.

Moss, B. (2002) *Working with Loss: A Training Resource Pack*. Learning Curve Publishing.

Murphy, M. (1996) *The Child Protection Unit.* Avebury.

Murphy, M. (2000) The Interagency Trainer, in Charles, M. and Hendry, E. (2000).

Murphy, M. (2004) *Working Together in Child Protection.* 2nd edn., Russell House Publishing.

Neighbourhood Renewal Unit and Regional Co-ordination Unit (2001) *Collaboration and Coordination in Area-based Initiatives.* NRU.

Newell, J. (2001) Breaking Down Barriers Between Young people and Employment. *Community Care.* 29 March.

Payne, M. (2000) *Teamwork in Multiprofessional Care.* Palgrave Macmillan.

Philpot, T. (2001) The Promised Land. *Community Care.* 8 March.

Piaget, J. and Inhelder, B. (1966) *The Psychology of the Child.* Routledge.

Pitts, J. (2000) The New Youth Justice and the Politics of Electoral Anxiety, in Goldson, B. (2000).

Pitts, J. (2002) Draft of paper scheduled for publication in *Research Matters.* July.

Pledger, B. (2001) How to Manage Endings. *Voluntary Action Manchester Newsletter.* March/April.

Powell, M., Exworthy, M. and Berney, L. (2001) Playing the Game of Partnership, in Sykes, R. et al. (2001).

Revans, L. (2001) Community Groups Fear 'Single Pot' Will End Social Regeneration Funding. *Community Care.* 13 December.

Rickford, F. (2000) We Will Survive. *Community Care.* 31 August.

Rickford, F. (2001) Dragon Slayer. *Community Care.* 19 April.

Roaf, C. (2002) *Coordinating Services for Included Children: Joined up Action.* Open University Press.

Saylor, S. (1992) *Catilina's Riddle.* Robinson.

SEU (2000) *National Strategy for Neighbourhool Renewal: A Framework for Consultation.* SEU.

SEU (2000) March. *A Report of Policy Action Team 12. Young People.* SEU.

Subhra, G. (2001) Reclaiming the Evaluation Agenda, in Factor, F. et al. (2001).

Sullivan, H. and Skelcher, C. (2002) *Working Across Boundaries: Collaboration in Public Services.* Palgrave Macmillan.

Sykes, R., Bochel, C. and Ellison, N. (Eds.) (2001) *Social Policy Review 13: Developments and Debates: 2000-2001.* The Policy Press.

Tennyson, R. (1998) *Managing Partnerships: Tools for Mobilising the Public Sector, Business and Civil Society as Partners in Development.* Prince of Wales Business Leaders Forum.

Tennyson, R. and Wilde, L. (2000) *The Guiding Hand: Brokering Partnerships for Sustainable Development,* The Prince of Wales Business Leaders Forum and the United Nations Staff College.

Thompson, N. (1999) *Stress Matters.* Pepar Publications.

Thompson, N. (2000a) *Understanding Social Work: Preparing for Practice.* Palgrave Macmillan.

Thompson, N. (2000b) *Theory and Practice in Human Services.* 2nd edn., Open University Press.

Thompson, N. (2000c) *Tackling Bullying and Harassment in the Workplace.* Pepar.

Thompson, N. (2002) *People Skills.* 2nd edn., Palgrave Macmillan.

Thompson, N. (2003a) *Promoting Equality: Challenging Discrimination and Oppression.* 2nd edn. Palgrave Macmillan.

Thompson, N. (2003b) *Communication and Language: A Handbook of Theory and Practice.* Palgrave Macmillan.

Thompson, N, Murphy, M. and Stradling, S. (1994) *Dealing with Stress.* Palgrave Macmillan.

Thompson, N, Murphy, M. and Stradling, S. (1996) *Meeting the Stress Challenge.* Russell House Publishing.

Walker, S. (2003) *Working Together for Healthy Young Minds.* Russell House Publishing.

Weiss, J. (1981) Substance vs Symbol in Administative Reform: The Case of Human Services Coordination. *Policy Analysis.* 7: 1, 21-45.

Wellard, S. (2000) One Bold Step for a Social Services Director. *Community Care.* 5 October.

Wheal, A. (2000) *Working With Parents: Learning From Other People's Experience.* Russell House Publishing.

White, K. and Grove, M. (2000) Towards an Understanding of Partnership. *NCVCCO Outlook.* Issue 7.

Winchester, R. (2000) Opportunities Knock. *Community Care.* 3 August.